Tales from the
BACK BUMPER

 BC 2685
 B.C. 3646 1913
 BC 1914 3646
 B.C. 1915 228
 B.C. 1916 7646

 7646 1919
BC 1920 4778
BC 1921 23632
BC 1922 29164
BC 1923 17412

27-216 26 BRITISH COLUMBIA
7-498 27 BRITISH COLUMBIA
389 28 BRITISH COLUMBIA
45-069 29 BRITISH COLUMBIA
47-746 3 BRITISH COLUMBIA

180 33 BRITISH COLUMBIA
68-040 34 BRITISH COLUMBIA
50-913 35 BRITISH COLUMBIA
64-563 36 BRITISH COLUMBIA
595 BRITISH COLUMBI

-1-558 40 BRITISH COLUMBIA
-1-558 41 BRITISH COLUMBIA
57-865 42 BRITISH COLUMBIA
53-732 43 BRITISH COLUMBIA
55-831 BRITISH COLUMBIA

J2-504 47 BRITISH COLUMBIA
1-779 48 BRITISH COLUMBIA
68-096 49 BRITISH COLUMBIA
44-448 50 BRITISH COLUMBIA
217-639 BRITISH·51·COLUMBI

796E 54 BRITISH COLUMBIA
172-111 BRITISH COLUMBIA · 55
84 BRITISH COLUMBIA 56
80 BRITISH COLUMBIA · 57
BRITISH COLUMBIA 82 1858 – CENTENARY – 19

410 BRITISH COLUMBIA 61
410 BRITISH COLUMBIA 62
11 BRITISH COLUMBIA 63
BEAUTIFUL 22-026 BRITISH COLUMBIA 64
BEAUTIFUL 6 88 BRITISH COLUMBIA

19 BEAUTIFUL 68 199-305 BRITISH COLUMBIA
19 BEAUTIFUL 69 97 BRITISH COLUMBIA
BEAUTIFUL BJK·111 BRITISH COLUMBIA
 BEAUTIFUL RGE·434 BRITISH COLUMBIA
 BEAUTIFUL ADJ-459 BRITISH COLUMB

Tales from the
BACK BUMPER

A CENTURY OF BC LICENCE PLATES

Christopher Garrish

VICTORIA · VANCOUVER · CALGARY

Heritage House Publishing Company Ltd.
heritagehouse.ca

LIBRARY AND ARCHIVES CANADA CATALOGUING IN PUBLICATION

Garrish, Christopher
    Tales from the back bumper: a century of BC licence plates / Christopher Garrish.

Includes bibliographical references and index.
Also issued in electronic format.

ISBN 978-1-927527-03-0

    1. Automobile licence plates—British Columbia—History.   2. Automobile licence plates—British Columbia—Miscellanea.   I. Title.

HE5620.L5G37 2013   388.3'422   C2012-906247-2

Edited by Lara Kordic
Proofread by Audrey McClellan
Cover and book design by Jacqui Thomas
Front cover photos courtesy of: Wayne Leidenfrost / *Vancouver Province*; Unknown / TB Vets Charitable Foundation;
    Art Jones photo, Vancouver Public Library 41157; and Deni Eagland / *Vancouver Sun*
Back cover photos courtesy of: City of Vancouver Archives, CVA 1184-48, Jack Lindsey; and Wallace Family
The author has made every effort to locate and obtain permission from the copyright holders of the photos in this book.
    If you find an error or omission, please contact the author via the publisher.

This book was produced using FSC®-certified, acid-free paper,
processed chlorine free and printed with vegetable-based inks.

Heritage House acknowledges the financial support for its publishing program from the Government of Canada through the Canada Book Fund (CBF) and Canada Council for the Arts, and from the province of British Columbia through the British Columbia Arts Council and the Book Publishing Tax Credit.

17 16 15 14 13   1 2 3 4 5

Printed in China

BEAUTIFUL CONTENTS
BRITISH COLUMBIA

Register of Permits
Motor Vehicles
issued under the
"Motor Vehicles Speed Regulation Act"
1904.

To **K8** (Kate),

3MM4 (Emma)

and **H347HER** (Heather)

ACKNOWLEDGEMENTS

The idea that it might actually be possible to write a history of British Columbia through the lens of the province's licence plates occurred to me about 12 years ago when I was working my way through graduate school. In researching my thesis topic (the co-operative marketing system instituted by Okanagan fruit growers), I spent a lot of time digging through various archives, libraries and microfilm collections across the province. On occasion, and to lighten the tone of the material I was sifting through, I would search "licence plates" to see what might be found.

Much to my surprise, these records were readily available, if not always complete, and I began to slowly assemble enough material for the outline of a good, if somewhat quirky, story. Turning this idea into reality, however, proved a far more daunting task than I had imagined, and it required the help of numerous people along the way.

Foremost amongst these are my fellow BC licence plate enthusiasts, who have spent many more years than I collecting, trading and preserving these rectangular pieces of metal. Three people in particular—Dave Hollins, Pierre Delacôte and Ron Garay—have shared their vast knowledge on the subject as well as the jewels of their collections, many of which appear on the following pages. Tom Lindner, a dedicated supporter of my website, BCpl8s.ca, as well as Bill Hobbis, Neale Hankins, Jon Ilnytzky, Rick Pilotte, John Roberts, Graham Casey, Dallas

Doyle, Don Schneider, Gerry Harrison, Gary Spicer and Bill McLellan, have also shared many stories and insights acquired over decades of collecting.

I also owe the fine folks at ICBC involved with the registration of motor vehicles a debt of gratitude for putting up with my persistent "fan boy" enthusiasm and interest in their work, particularly Jeannie Lee, George Power, Rob Termuende and Adam Grossman.

Then there is the legion of individuals who, rather unexpectedly and very unselfishly, gave their time freely to help with the writing of this book—particularly Keith Jackman and Ron Marston, formerly of the Motor Vehicle Branch; George Piva with Astrographic Industries Ltd.; Neil Mackie and the TB Vets; and Archie Steacy of the BC Veterans Commemorative Association and Sharel Fraser, formerly of Veterans Affairs. Andrew Osborne, James Douglas Moore and my brother, Matthew "Buck" Garrish, had the particularly enjoyable task of slogging through early drafts of the book and providing feedback. Of course, "Family and Friends" (that other great, but less well-publicized provincial "Circle Route") put me up and helped facilitate the research of this book in Vancouver and Victoria. I know there are many others not listed here, but whose contributions appear throughout the book and are equally appreciated!

If not for Rodger Touchie and Vivian Sinclair at Heritage House seeing something in a story about licence plates, this would still be only an idea inside my head. Thanks also to Kate Scallion and my editor, Lara Kordic, for whipping this book into shape, and Jacqui Thomas for coming up with a fantastic layout.

Finally, I want to acknowledge the very enlightened approach adopted by the City of Vancouver Archives in "making the materials in its holding available to as large a community as possible, without any unwarranted restrictions as to their use"! As someone who resides in the Interior of the province, where easy access to major archival collections is difficult, the city's open-sourced, web-based system of access, particularly to its historical photographs, has made important material available that might not otherwise have found its way into this book—so, thank you.

FOREWORD

The ordinary things in life help define us. Things we take for granted only become noticeable when someone holds them before us and says, "Look at this." That is exactly what Christopher Garrish has done with *Tales from the Back Bumper: A Century of BC Licence Plates.*

When I was growing up, the presentation of the new licence plate was always an anticipated event. I still remember the green-and-gold plate that marked BC's 100th birthday in 1958. In those days, the licence plate was noticed. Not so much today.

Nowadays, like most people, I ponder my licence plate once a year when I place my new insurance decal on it. But as I wandered through the pages of *Back Bumper,* I realized that it is the licence plate's somewhat unassuming place in our lives that adds to its importance as a mirror of time and place.

While I was premier, the Province introduced two specialty plates to celebrate two distinct aspects of our province. The first was a Veterans plate to commemorate the sacrifice and commitment of our men and women in uniform. It was a good idea—a daily reminder of their service. I am always pleased to see one of those plates that now adorn the cars of the young and the old. That licence plate is a reminder to us all and makes a difference to our veterans. The second was an Olympic plate launched in advance of the 2010 Winter Games. When the "Best Place on Earth" plate was launched, I thought it was straightforward enough—a slogan that captured a place with natural endowments too numerous to count, a place of opportunity that had created a richly diverse, peaceful, multicultural, multi-dimensional society. BC certainly seemed like the best place on earth to me.

Our licence plates are touchstones for our memories and reflections of who we are. They say something about us, sometimes without our knowing it. *Tales from the Back Bumper* is fun, and it's nostalgic. I hope you enjoy the ride.

Gordon Campbell
High Commission for Canada to the United Kingdom
and former premier of British Columbia (2001–2011)

The ABC-123 of LICENCE PLATES

My first licence plate? Well, that came off the back of my grandmother's car on a family visit to Vancouver during the summer of Expo 86. The government was keen to see the newly designed licence plates, which incorporated a cutting-edge provincial flag design, displayed on all vehicles, and motorists were required to replace their old blue-and-white plates, which had been in use since 1979. In exchange for switching over my grandmother's plates, she let me keep her old set, which came complete with an expiration decal that incorporated the stylized Expo 86 logo in place of the year. For a 12-year-old boy, this was definitely cooler than any souvenir from one of the numerous gift shops that littered the grounds of the Expo site.

That I would be drawn to a dirty old licence plate is not all that surprising. As a child, I had always been intrigued by plates, probably because of a game my parents devised to occupy my brother and me on an earlier road trip to Vancouver, which took us through the United States in late summer of 1980. The task was simple enough; every time my brother or I saw a new licence plate, we had to colour squares in a notebook to match it and write down the state or province it came from. Later, gazing at licence plates helped me survive endless family Sunday drives, and over the years I would come across odd licence plates

★ A plate that would go unloved by most collectors is the first and most cherished plate in this writer's collection.

and hang them on the wall beside my 1986 British Columbia plate. Collecting plates remained a casual pastime until a random search on the Internet one day in the late 1990s revealed a whole community of like-minded individuals. For years, I thought I was the only one who saw the intrinsic merit and joy in collecting licence plates. Now, from fewer than a dozen plates, I was quickly able to acquire examples from each of the provinces as well as the beginnings of a "birth year" run. I soon taught myself some basic HTML skills and created a website to present my growing collection and its colourful history. This would eventually morph into BCpl8s.ca—a quirky, award-winning website detailing the peculiarities from 100 years of licence plate use in British Columbia.

While my site receives modest traffic, it generates a steady stream of questions from visitors who are curious to know how much a particular plate might be worth, who it might have been registered to or where they might be able to purchase a set of BC plates of their own. Yet, every once in a while, a question will leave me completely flummoxed. Take this head-scratcher: "Did the Romans require licence plates on chariots?" While some websites suggest that chariots did need to be registered 2,000 years ago, there is no evidence to suggest that they were also required to display a licence plate. But, if not, then when and where were the first licence plates issued, and why?

Most collectors believe that licence plates emerged in late-17th-century Europe, when owners of horse-drawn carriages were required to register them with authorities and display registration "badges" or "discs" that were affixed to the interior and/or exterior of the carriage. In France, carriage registration became mandatory during the reign of Louis XIV (1638-1715) so that those who caused accidents could be identified and apprehended. As so few people could read or write in this era, a drawing or emblem was the principal form of identification. By the 1780s, as the system of licensing became more formalized, a government edict forced French carriage drivers to attach a metal plate to their vehicles that included the name and address of the vehicle's owner.[1] In the United Kingdom, carts licensed for hire in London were required to display brass plates with the city's coat of arms and a number as early as 1681. The London Hackney Carriage Act of 1831 stated that stage coaches were required to be "duly licensed and having proper numbered plates."[2] By the end of the 19th century, jurisdictions throughout Europe were issuing various types of badges and ovals for use on horse-drawn carriages, a practice that had also been carried over to certain North American cities.

The Europeans, particularly the French, were also leading the world in the production of gasoline-powered automobiles at this time. Early adopters of this new mode of transportation, the French were the first to require permits to operate vehicles in 1891, as well as the first to require licence plates when the City of Paris mandated their use in 1893.[3] North Americans began to realize the need for licence plates about a decade later, when automobiles became more commonplace in the United States and Canada.[4] In fact, the term "licence plate" is a misnomer that harkens back to this period, when it was vehicles that were licensed as opposed to drivers.[5] The first North American jurisdiction to require them was New York State in 1901. Vehicle owners made their own plates and inscribed them with their own initials, which was thought to facilitate the identification of drivers and make them more accountable for their actions behind the wheel. Unfortunately, by 1903, it was apparent that many owners were displaying fake initials or using their own without actually registering, which prompted the state to change to a numerical system.[6]

The first government-issued—as opposed to homemade—plates appeared in Massachusetts in 1903, and eight years later Ontario became the first Canadian jurisdiction to issue standardized plates. By 1918, all 48 of the continental United States and a majority of the nine Canadian provinces were issuing standardized licence plates.[7]

A wide variety of materials has been used in the production of licence plates, with rubber, leather, wood and even canvas popular in the era when

★ An example of an early issue licence plate from the State of New York. These plates were required to be made by the vehicle owner and were to display the owner's initials for easy identification. This plate was made by Edward F. Low of 200 Broadway in New York City after he registered his vehicle in 1903.

STEVE RAICHE
WWW.LEATHERLICENSEPLATES.COM

No Licence Plates Required

Unlike many US states that have the tradition of awarding "license" plate number 1 to the governor, in British Columbia the head of the provincial government is not even required to use a licence plate. In a parliamentary democracy, this is not the premier (the leader of the largest party in the legislature), but the lieutenant-governor (LG), who represents the queen when she is out of the province—which is basically all the time. Despite being the constitutional source of all state power in the province, the lieutenant-governor's role is largely symbolic and generally confined to that of goodwill ambassador. Performing this ceremonial role is undoubtedly demanding; however, it is not without its own interesting set of perquisites, one of which is the ability to drive around the province without a licence plate. This dates back to December 21, 1926, when the provincial government was advised that "his Honour the Lieutenant-Governor (Robert Bruce) is dispensing with ordinary plates issued under the 'Motor Vehicle Act'. In lieu of these his automobiles will carry a metal shield in front of the radiator bearing the crest of British Columbia." This decision came about because the requirement to register a vehicle and display licence plates was interpreted as a tax (or road-user charge), and as the queen could not be taxed, the requirement to display licence plates on the LG's vehicle was deemed invalid.

It was eventually determined, likely in the 1970s, that the risk of driving the LG in an uninsured vehicle was too great, and the vehicles were formally registered and issued a pair of standard passenger licence plates (stored in the glovebox).[8]

★ The design of the plate has changed over the years, and the LG actually employs two different designs on official vehicles. On the more formal vehicle that is used to transport the LG to the opening of the legislature, a crest incorporating the provincial shield of arms surrounded by a circlet of 10 gold stylized maple leaves representing the ten provinces of Canada is displayed (top). The touring vehicle, which is used to travel to events across the province, displays the provincial coat of arms (bottom).

motorists had to provide their own plates. When states and provinces took over the production and issuance of licence plates, steel plates with a porcelain cover were the most common, but these gave way to basic steel plates in later decades. In times when steel supplies were restricted, principally during the First and Second World Wars, other materials such as wood, soybean, cardboard, tin, copper, brass and even plastic were used to make licence plates. Today, aluminum is the material of choice in North America.[9] Throughout Europe and parts of Asia, motorists still provide their own licence plates; small businesses make the plates to a certain specification set by the state. In Germany this approach works quite well, but in countries such as India, authorities have launched a campaign against "fancy number plates" featuring decorative fonts and scripts in all manner of shapes, sizes and colours, which are very difficult to read.[10]

Basic licence plate design initially changed little from decade to decade: a dual colour scheme, embossed letters and the occasional slogan punctuated by a simple logo appeared on most licence plates through the 1950s. Of course, there were notable exceptions where states issued elaborately embossed logos or applied colourful decals to the middle of their plates.

The dual colour scheme approach began to change after the US federal government mandated the use of reflective sheeting on licence plates in the mid-1960s.[11] This allowed law enforcement officials to more easily identify vehicles at night and helped reduce nighttime traffic accidents by allowing motorists to see other vehicles.[12] The new reflective sheeting also substantially increased the number and palette of colours that could be applied to a licence plate.[13] In

★ The first "graphic" licence plate, from South Dakota in 1974, depicted Mount Rushmore.

★ Elaborately embossed licence plate designs included the 1917 Arizona steer head, the 1928 Idaho potato and the 1947 Idaho and 1958 Colorado skier plates. In later years, colourful decals were applied to the middle of some states' licence plates, including a peach on the 1941 Georgia and a potato on the 1948 Idaho.

GARY FOX (1917 ARIZONA)

⋆ An assortment of new graphic licence plates that appeared in 1976 to commemorate the US Bicentennial.

1974, South Dakota issued the first graphic licence plate, which incorporated a screened image of Mount Rushmore. Following this lead, a number of other states began to introduce ever more elaborately designed licence plates ahead of the American Bicentennial in 1976.

In the wake of the 1986 *Challenger* space shuttle disaster, the Florida legislature created a special licence plate that motorists could purchase for an extra fee of 17 dollars.[14] It was a runaway success—sales quickly paid for the construction of an Astronaut Memorial at the Kennedy Space Center and have continued to fund space-related programs in the state ever since.

⋆ The first "specialty" licence plate, the 1987 Florida *Challenger* plate.

Florida's success was not lost on the other states, and only a few short years later the Texas state legislature considered creating a specialty plate made of custom bronze with 14-karat gold-plated letters and numbers. Costing $1,000 each, the plates were envisioned as a "sure fire money maker" in the midst of a sagging economy.[15] While the proposal never made it beyond the concept stage, it is emblematic of the "gold rush" mentality that has gripped organizations and governments across the United States when it comes to the revenue-generating potential of these specialty licence plates. Some states have reduced the concept to the absurd; Maryland, for example, offers its motorists a choice from around 800 different themes.[16] An important consideration in the creation of any specialty plate is the design, as the look of the plate is sometimes as important as the cause that is being promoted.[17] The apex of this trend was reached in 1996 with Pennsylvania's Flagship *Niagara* licence plate.

This was the first time a full-colour painting—*The Battle of Lake Erie*, by Julian O. Davidson—had ever been reproduced on a licence plate.[18] It was also one of the first times that a plate design came at the expense of the registration number. Law enforcement officials in Pennsylvania complained that the painting's "vivid strokes and dark colours" obscured the state name and nearly every other aspect of the plate that was important for identification purposes.[19] These competing demands of legibility, visual attractiveness and fundraising objectives continue to drive trends in licence plate design. Computers are now capable of printing "flat" (un-embossed) plates on demand and with even greater image quality, while more and more organizations and businesses are seeking to sponsor their own visually unique licence plates in order to raise funds.

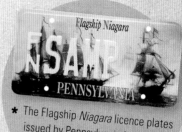

★ The Flagship *Niagara* licence plates issued by Pennsylvania in 1996.

As the number of vehicles in British Columbia continued to increase over the decades, so did the size and operation of the department responsible for their registration. Having grown from a small office in the Provincial Police offices at the courthouse in Bastion Square, Victoria, the Motor Vehicle Branch (MVB) was transferred to the Attorney General's Department in 1945. The MVB would handle the bulk of motor vehicle registration and issuance of licence plates over the next half-century until it was amalgamated with the Insurance Corporation of British Columbia (ICBC) in 1996. ICBC issues approximately 1.5 million (or 750,000 sets) of licence plates each year for all types of vehicles. To ensure that sufficient supplies are always on hand, ICBC advises its manufacturer, currently Waldale Industries of Nova Scotia, of its projected requirements every September. A purchase order to Waldale, along with the required sequences to appear on the plates, is sent only two months before ICBC anticipates it will require the stock. When these orders come in, they are warehoused in Burnaby before being shipped to the various Autoplan agents located throughout the province. Some agencies, such as the AllWest Insurance outlet on Burrard Street in Vancouver, can go through a pallet of licence plates in a month (a pallet holds between 40 and 50 boxes with 25 plate sets in a box), whereas other brokers might only require five boxes, or as few as one box in a month.

★ The 2010 Winter Games licence plate, introduced by ICBC in 2007, was the first specialty licence plate issued in British Columbia available to all motorists willing to pay an extra 35 dollars. The plates proved wildly successful, which can partially be attributed to the longevity of the current flag design, which has been issued to motorists since 1985.

Shortages do happen on occasion, but these are usually related to internal decisions. Take, for instance, the runaway success of the 2010 Winter Games

★ In the 1970s, scuba divers in Kalamalka Lake recovered a number of crates containing unissued 1930 passenger plates originating from the Vernon office of the MVB. One can only imagine the unceremonious end that befell these plates!

specialty licence plate, which caught ICBC by surprise. When the initial order for the plates was placed in 2006, it was anticipated that 250,000 sets would meet demand over the three years the plates were to be offered for sale. After the plates started flying out of Autoplan agencies, ICBC was faced with the dilemma of placing a second order and potentially being left with dead stock, or running the risk of not having enough stock and missing out on possible sales before the end of the program in December 2010. Staff ultimately decided to juggle stock, recall excess inventory and redistribute these plates to Autoplan agencies where demand was stronger.[20]

Once upon a time, staff members at the various MVB offices throughout the province were simply required to submit a declaration to the Superintendent of Provincial Police at the end of the licensing year stating that all surplus licence plate stock had been destroyed. How they disposed of these plates was left to the discretion of the individual. One of the most dramatic, if not environmentally sensitive methods, which has become the stuff of legends, was that of the officer in Trail, who would take the box of surplus licence plates to the centre point of the Old Trail Bridge and (un)ceremoniously hurl them into the Columbia River below. The odd plate still washes up on shore to this day. At one point, it was possible to obtain returned licence plates from the firm contracted to recycle them, until one of these plates ended up on a getaway car involved in a criminal activity in the United States. After this, ICBC changed contractors and instituted a double-entry accounting system to ensure that no returned plates went astray.

By their nature, licence plates lend themselves to a very linear type of history in which there is a clearly identifiable start date—invariably the first year plates were issued—and a corresponding end date, which could be anything from the introduction of a new design or a new serial format to the phasing out of a particular plate type. This tends to encourage licence plate enthusiasts to focus on the more arcane aspects of licence plates such as colours, materials, the font used on the dies, the number of plates issued in any given year and even the placement and spacing of boltholes. While this type of information is like catnip for collectors, and tends to dominate the pages of websites devoted to licence plate history (and BCpl8s.ca is no exception), the history presented here is different. It eschews neat chronological lines and presents the stories of these rectangular pieces of aluminum that we attach to our vehicles in a series of themes that will roam back and forth across the decades of the 20th century and into the first decade of the 21st century. There is also a certain hierarchy to the presentation of the material in this book, one that should be readily apparent to anyone who has dabbled in licence plate collecting. Passenger plates are the most commonly issued type of plate in any jurisdiction, and they are usually the main focus of collectors attempting to put together a province or state "run." After this come the non-passenger, or "oddball," plate types such as motorcycle, dealer, truck, trailer, samples, prorated, and so on. The first chapters of this book deal with passenger plate trends, whereas later chapters delve into more obscure areas such as quarterly logging truck, municipal and motor carrier licence plates. I hope that you will come to share some of my enthusiasm for BC licence plates and that "plate spotting" will become an entertaining diversion as you drive the roads of this province.

2 PRESSING PROBLEMS

For the first half-dozen years of the 20th century, the automobile was very much an oddity in British Columbia, and its future seemed uncertain. A Vancouver engineering firm had an early version of a truck that could haul machinery down to the docks. The local roads, however, were so rough that the vehicle "shook to bits" and was abandoned. In 1899, the Vancouver firm of Armstrong, Morrison & Company imported a Stanley Steamer car and planned to reproduce it in their shops and sell versions to the local market. But before production could begin, the shops were sold and the new owners chose not to pursue automobile manufacturing.

It would be another three years before the first automobile arrived on Vancouver Island: Dr. E.C. Hart imported a single-cylinder Oldsmobile on May 24, 1902, at a cost of $900 (the equivalent of roughly $24,000 today). After the vehicle was unloaded from a crate at the E&N Station in Victoria, Hart proceeded to drive up Johnson Street, which was "tough

★ The first horseless carriage ever seen on the streets of Vancouver, owned by the late W.H. Armstrong (circa 1899).

CITY OF VANCOUVER ARCHIVES, CVA 677-70, PHILLIP TIMMS

going because crowds of people ranged in front and gawked as they had never seen anything like it."[1] A few years later, the public mood shifted from fascination to annoyance, and the provincial legislature felt compelled to pass the first Act to Regulate the Speed and Operation of Motor Vehicles on Highways in 1904, even though there were no more than 32 vehicles in BC that year.

As automobiles became more popular across North America, accidents and mayhem followed in their wake. One story that circulated in the US held that when the number of automobiles in Missouri numbered only four, two of them managed to collide on a St. Louis street with such force that both drivers were injured.[2] In BC, the new legislation attempted to address some of these concerns by requiring basic safety equipment, such as warning signals, lights and a speed limit of 10 miles per hour in cities and 15 miles per hour in rural areas.[3] The Superintendent of Provincial Police was in charge of ensuring that drivers were following the new speed limits and other regulations. This meant that motorists now had to register their automobiles with the superintendent's office and, in return, he would issue them a number and record their details in an official register. At the time, the Victoria office of the Provincial Police was located in the basement office of the courthouse in Bastion Square at Langley Street. In order to register vehicles in the Victoria area, a constable would take the register, stand on Langley Street, stop each automobile that came along and inquire if the driver had paid for his licence. If the driver responded "no," the officer would request the two-dollar fee on the spot and write out a receipt. The receipt number became the automobile's registration number, and the driver was expected to have this number made into a single licence plate that would be displayed on the back of the vehicle.[4]

The new legislation set out a few basic requirements for licence plates, but motorists were free to use any material that

★ At Beacon Hill, May 24, 1905—"We are not quite reconciled to the Automobiles. They alarm the horses; the horses alarm the ladies; the ladies alarm the babies; the babies alarm the dogs, and much general confusion ensues." The "new" May Day as seen by Emily Carr.[5]

★ A copy of Permit No. 1 issued under the Motor Vehicle Speed Regulation Act on February 29, 1904, to John Barnsley of Victoria.
IMAGE MS-2661 COURTESY OF ROYAL BC MUSEUM, BC ARCHIVES

★ In this photo, a BC Express Company vehicle is shown transporting goods into the interior of the province. It is thought that the plate displayed on the rear of the vehicle is made of painted wood or metal. The company was issued registration Nos. 1122 and 1123 on August 6, 1910.
VANCOUVER PUBLIC LIBRARY, 8336

★ To help with identification "at any time after dusk and before dawn," motorists were also required to display their licence plate number on a lamp attached to their vehicle. In the above image, the number 85 is clearly visible on the driver's side lamp. The number was issued to Dr. A.R. Baker on June 11, 1906. **CITY OF VANCOUVER ARCHIVES, TRANS P55, JAMES MATTHEWS**

★ Registration number 1143 was issued on August 11, 1910, to W. Kilray of Vancouver and is the typical piece of leather with affixed house numbers and letters.

they wished. Joseph Morris, who had the first registration number in Alberta, opted to display the number by vertically attaching a broom handle on the rear of his vehicle. Local authorities tried to prosecute him for the improper display of a licence plate, but he was able to convince the presiding judge that the broom handle met the requirements of Alberta's Automobile Act.[6] While British Columbia motorists from this period were not quite as inventive, they did make licence plates out of wood (planks, not broomsticks), canvas, metal and, most commonly, leather. A rectangular piece of leather could easily be obtained from the local horse stable, and house numbers and letters could be purchased from the corner hardware store and affixed later.

One of the problems in allowing people to produce their own plates, apart from the lack of uniformity in design, was that the plates displayed no expiration date. A homemade licence plate could conceivably be used for years without any way for the police to easily identify a valid registration—which also made the identification of "blacklisted" drivers extremely difficult in an era before drivers were licensed. With the number of registered vehicles nearing 4,250, the Motor Traffic Regulation Act (1911) was amended, and responsibility for the production and distribution of licence plates was transferred to the Province effective March 1, 1913. From that point on, plates would be issued annually, display different colours than the year before, include an expiry date and be mounted on both the front and rear of a vehicle. These new regulations would allow the Provincial Police to keep better track of the number of vehicles being registered and make it difficult for people to shirk their registration fees, which had been increased to 10 dollars for all vehicles.

Provincial procurement regulations stipulated that plates had to be sourced in British Columbia. If this was not possible, the plates would be purchased from elsewhere in Canada before consideration could be given to a US company.[7] Two Ontario firms, the MacDonald Manufacturing Company of Toronto and the McClary Manufacturing Company of London, were dominating the field of licence plate production in this era, and both would be shortlisted to become the official plate producers for BC. McClary had already produced Ontario's first standardized licence plates in 1911 and was the supplier to all of the western provinces when Superintendent Colin S. Campbell of the Provincial Police, began searching for a manufacturer to meet BC's growing need.

Better known for its production of household appliances such as stoves, McClary employed very similar techniques to make licence plates, using a heavy-gauge piece of steel with a baked porcelain enamel cover. When the first shipment of plates arrived from McClary, staff at the Provincial Police office in Victoria discovered that the shipping crates had been overloaded and were impossible to lift. As the office was below street level, a window was opened and a greased plank was used to slide the boxes in for stacking. The weight of the boxes sent them crashing through the wood floor of the office, which then had to be replaced at some cost to the police.[8]

★ The McClary Manufacturing Company showed a distinct lack of originality when producing licence plates for Ontario (1911), Manitoba (1911), Saskatchewan (1912), Alberta (1912) and British Columbia (1913).

Licence to Travel   For collector Ron Garay, one of the most interesting "British Columbia" licence plates he has acquired in over 20 years of collecting is one that was produced by the Automobile Club of Southern California in 1910.

The porcelain plate, known within the hobby as a "dog-bone" because of its shape, turned up in a Fraser Valley barn in the 1990s and eventually made its way to Garay. Curious about the history of the plate and how it came to be in the province, Garay contacted a fellow collector in California, who advised that records held at the State Archives indicated the number—31214—had been registered to A.E. Todd of Victoria.

An Internet search revealed that Todd (also known as "Good Roads Todd") served a term as mayor of Victoria, was the sponsor of a gold medal presented to the first person to successfully drive across Canada and spent his honeymoon driving from Tijuana, Mexico, to Vancouver to promote the construction of a highway along the Pacific coast.

Under the rules of the day, Todd had to register his vehicle in California in order to use the state's road system, and to display his new California registration number he ordered porcelain licence plates that the Automobile Club of Southern California provided to its members for a fee of one dollar.

★ Shown at left is A.E. Todd in 1910 with California licence plate No. 31214 clearly visible on the back of the vehicle. Above, Ron Garay holds this same licence plate over one hundred years later. **CITY OF VICTORIA ARCHIVES, M01052**

To compound the administrative burden associated with the distribution of the new plates, Campbell directed his constables to issue new registrants only one plate from the new pairs of 1913 porcelain plates until the legislature amended the Motor Traffic Regulation Act.[9] This way, motorists would not suffer the expense of having to purchase leather plates for new vehicles only months before they became obsolete. Of course, when the amendments to the act were adopted and annual registration became mandatory, constables all over the province found themselves having to track down motorists with only a single 1913 plate to ensure they were properly registered and displaying the other plate on the front of their vehicles.[10]

Months after the new licence plates were issued, many vehicle owners began to complain that the porcelain chipped very easily and became disfigured. Curious as to how other jurisdictions had dealt with this problem, Campbell contacted his counterparts in other provinces and states to inquire about materials, manufacturers and costs.

The Illinois secretary of state recommended the Adams Seal & Stamp Company of St. Louis, Missouri, but provincial purchasing requirements all but guaranteed that the 1914 contract would again be awarded to McClary. The Ontario manufacturer attempted to address some of the concerns with the quality of the plates by offering to move the location of the boltholes and reinforce them with lead washers. Material shortages caused by the outbreak of war in Europe prompted Campbell to award the 1915 contract to the MacDonald Manufacturing Company of Toronto, which produced lithographed flat steel plates that were lighter and used fewer materials than porcelain plates.[11]

★ When the new plates arrived from McClary Manufacturing it was discovered that not only had the series provided to automobile dealerships (characterized by a D prefix) been produced in sets of five matching numbers, but the letters "BC" identifying the issuing jurisdiction had been forgotten. These problems were rectified on the 1914 licence plates.

★ One of the problems with porcelain licence plates is that they easily chip and fracture. It is not known if the damage done to this 1914 plate was incurred during its time on a vehicle or from subsequent storage.

★ The 1914 No. 218 (top left) is an example of the porcelain plates made by the McClary Manufacturing Company for British Columbia between 1913 and 1914. ★ The MacDonald Manufacturing Company of Toronto produced the 1914 Alberta licence plate (middle left). Material shortages during the First World War and chipping problems associated with porcelain led the Alberta Deputy Provincial Secretary to recommend MacDonald Manufacturing to the BC Superintendent of Provincial Police.
★ The original purchase order for the 1915 licence plates requested that the colour scheme "be bright and clean, that is the white a pure white, and the red brilliant, so that the numbers will show up distinctly"—similar to the 1913 Alberta licence plates (see page 40). MacDonald Manufacturing, however, could not produce red "markers" so they went with a dark green background (bottom left).[12]

During the three-year period in which MacDonald supplied the province, vehicle registrations increased by 57 percent, making the licence plate tender very lucrative. John Tacey of the Vancouver company J.R. Tacey & Son (a sheet metal manufacturing outfit) wanted to take advantage of the provincial purchasing rules and win the contract. Tacey travelled to Seattle in early 1917 to investigate a stamping machine used to make licence plates for Washington State. His plan was to purchase the machine, ship it to Vancouver and have the previous owners assist with the installation and tutor him in its operation. Unfortunately, the owners were German and considered to be "alien enemies" (because of Canada's participation in the First World War) and were barred from entering Canada. With few other options, Tacey was forced to bring the machine to Vancouver by himself and "sweat it out night and day to see how the thing ran." When the 1918 plate tender was issued, Tacey put his bid in, won and "proceeded to make them [the plates] quite well."[13]

★ While it remains unclear from the historical records if the machine that Tacey bought in Seattle in 1917 was the same used to produce earlier Washington State licence plates, there is a striking similarity between these and the 1918 BC plate. ★ The dies used on both plates are very similar as are the number and placement of the boltholes and slots, raised outer edge and overall dimensions (which, in this era, could vary wildly between jurisdictions).

As the only firm in the Dominion capable of manufacturing embossed licence plates, J.R. Tacey & Son won contracts in the Prairies and had designs on becoming the supplier for even more provinces. To ramp up production, Tacey got a loan from the Department of Industries in 1920 that allowed him to relocate to a larger facility and purchase new machinery, including a 200-cubic-foot electric oven for enamelling embossed licence plates (the largest of its kind in the country at that time).[14]

Tacey would continue to manufacture BC licence plates throughout the 1920s, but would eventually lose the contract for the 1930 series to the Thompson Heating & Ventilating Company, also of Vancouver. It is no coincidence that this change occurred at the same time as the election of a Conservative government under the leadership of Simon Fraser Tolmie in 1928. The president of the Thompson Company, George Thompson, also happened to be the head of the Ward Eleven Conservative Association in Vancouver.[15] The 1930 contract was valued in excess of $15,000.

Confident of obtaining future orders with the Tolmie administration, Thompson invested $6,000 in a new plant and equipment. Thompson could not have predicted the onset of the Great Depression, however, or Tolmie's attempt to deal with the crisis by slashing public expenditures. In an attempt to save $5,000, Tolmie announced that the 1931 licence plates would be produced at the Oakalla Prison Farm in Burnaby. This move opened a rift within the Tolmie administration, as Vancouver Conservatives felt the use of prison labour was contrary to the government's policy of encouraging local industry. Not only had the $15,000 loan that Tacey obtained from the previous Liberal administration of John Oliver in 1920 been forgiven, but the company was granted an un-tendered contract to install the equipment at Oakalla and supervise the manufacturing of 30,000 pairs of 1931 licence plates for $14,000.

★ Due to metal shortage associated with the Great War, the Province issued metal renewal tabs for the first time in 1919. By the end of that year, these shortages had become so severe that a printing company in the Marpole neighbourhood of Vancouver was contracted to make cardboard licence plates for new registrants.
PIERRE DELACÔTE

★ The Plate Shop at Oakalla (circa 1950s).

IMAGE I-49801 COURTESY OF ROYAL BC MUSEUM, BC ARCHIVES

The government justified the deal on the basis that the previous Liberal government had attempted to buy Tacey's equipment, but had been put off by the $70,000 asking price. The attorney general also stated that licence plate manufacturing was a "non-competitive" industry (despite the presence of both Thompson and Tacey in the Vancouver marketplace), while the Minister of Industries announced that the Sheet Metal Workers Union fully supported the move—a claim the union hotly denied.[16]

After a hearing of the Public Accounts Committee the following month, the Liberal member for Nanaimo, George Pearson, reported that the Conservative members of the committee agreed that Oakalla would have an advantage over a private firm as it did not have "to pay compensation if a convict worker crushed his hand in the machine." The Commissioner of Industries, Colonel D.B. Martin, conceded that Tacey's machinery was "old-fashioned" and that he was aware of complaints regarding its safety but was not aware of any accident within the past 10 years.[17] The province would learn the hard way that the motivations of a captive labour force are slightly different from those of workers engaged by private industry. During a shift at the Plate Shop, a prisoner purposely placed one of his hands into the press and activated the stamp. He allegedly lost a few fingers and possibly part of the hand and went on to sue the government for not taking the necessary steps to ensure the safety

★ Although J.R. Tacey & Son would alternate dies throughout the 1920s to frustrate counterfeiters, the "slanted" dies that appeared on the 1927 plates (top left) are commonly associated with Tacey's period of production. ★ Following the change of government in 1928 and the awarding of the 1930 plate contract to the Conservative-connected Thompson Heating & Ventilating Company, the dies used on this year's plate would appear this one time only (middle left). ★ With the acquisition of Tacey & Son's equipment by the province in 1930, the familiar "slanted" dies reappeared in 1931 (bottom left).

42-086 27
BRITISH COLUMBIA

36-349 -30
BRITISH COLUMBIA

37-486 31
BRITISH COLUMBIA

of the equipment. The government lost the case, and the injured party supposedly received a lifetime pension as a result of the "accident." To prevent similar injuries in the future, prisoners working the press were ordered to have a harness attached to their wrists to keep their hands away from the machine when it was in a downward motion. When the press went back up again, the inmate was free to change the die for the next plate.[18]

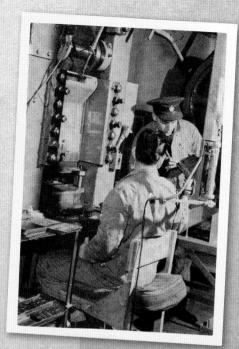

★ One of the original presses from Oakalla remains in use to this day. When Astrographic won the contract to produce British Columbia licence plates in 1984, the equipment was transferred from Oakalla to the Astrographic facility in Surrey, and it is still used today to produce licence plates for Yukon. Employees' hands are no longer tied to the equipment. Shown above are the last dies used to stamp out plates at Oakalla.

★ One of the few known pictures of the Plate Shop at Oakalla shows how the licence plate equipment worked. There appears to be an activation mechanism immediately behind the prisoner which required him to be sitting back in his chair before the machine would engage.
BC CORRECTIONS BRANCH HISTORICAL SOCIETY

Operating a manufacturing business out of a prison presented other challenges for the government. As one manager of the Plate Shop noted many years later, "in an operation such as ours we are not endeavouring to make money but to provide a programme for inmates and to develop good work habits."[19] Developing good work habits generated the occasional setback, and none was more spectacular than the fiasco that beset the 1948 licence plates.

★ The image shown is an example of a "defective" 1948 licence plate where the white topcoat has begun to wash off.

★ Starting in 1940, the MVB used letter prefixes so that five-digit licence plates could continue to be used, even though registrations now exceeded 100,000. An A prefix denoted Vancouver Island, B Vancouver, F New Westminster and H other Lower Mainland locations. The need to replace over 30,000 defective plates in 1948, combined with growth in automobile ownership, made it necessary to introduce additional letter prefixes, such as K, P, R, S, T, U and W.

As it did every January, the MVB began to ship allotments of the 1948 series to its offices around the province, as well as individual licence plate sets to certain people ahead of the March 1 licence year. By the end of the month, over 2,000 pairs had been sent out, and motorists could start purchasing the 1948 plates on February 2. On February 12, the *Vancouver Province* casually reported that a "gremlin had got into the white paint" used to highlight the numbers and letters and that 10 defective sets of licence plates had been discovered. The MVB launched an investigation and advised motorists with peeling plates to return them for a new set. Initially, the problem appeared to be confined to the first block of 1,000 plates (numbers 1 to 999) as well as those in the 7,000 and 8,000 series. Then the trickle turned into a torrent, and by the end of February the MVB office at West Georgia was receiving over 50 defective sets of plates a day. At this rate of return, the government would have to replace almost half of the 120,000 sets of plates that had been manufactured that year. The defective plates were fine until exposed to water, which rainy Vancouver presented in abundance. By the end of March, the rate of returned plates had hit 200 sets a day.[20]

Suspicions immediately turned to the inmates at Oakalla who manufactured the plates and the possibility that they had found a way to sabotage the 1948 series. Some thought the inmates had overheated the plates in the drying oven after the base coat had been applied, causing the plates to become too hard and preventing white topcoat from adhering properly. The Superintendent of Motor Vehicles, George Hood, laughed at suggestions of sabotage and attempted to deflect questions regarding quality control at the Plate Shop. "It's not the prisoners, it's not the paint," he said. "We don't know what is causing the rapid deterioration . . . [but] we've got scientists on the job now [and] perhaps they will solve the mystery." The British America Paint Company (BAPCO), which supplied the paint, advised the MVB that testing had not found any flaws. Without an official explanation, conspiracy theories emerged.

Some blamed it on "the secret, diabolical work of a maleficent Red agent who wanted to bring the capitalist Coalition government of BC into contempt." Others thought that radioactivity from nuclear testing in the United States had drifted north through the atmosphere and was coming down with the rain in Vancouver, eating the paint off the licence plates.[21]

No official explanation was ever offered, and approximately 30,000 licence plates had to be replaced. Today the popular belief is that the prisoners had been urinating into the paint batch, which would be consistent with some of the other hijinks that occurred within the Plate Shop. To allay any concerns that might arise with the 1949 series, Hood had the plates weather-tested in a machine that could simulate the equivalent of a year's weathering by subjecting the plates to cold, heat, rain, fog and ice—all in the span of two weeks. The superintendent reported that "as far as is humanly possible, I think I can say the paint won't peel this year."[22]

While nothing ever eclipsed the magnitude of the 1948 paint fiasco, MVB officials always had to be on guard for problems. A constant challenge was the delivery of the plates from Oakalla to the main offices in Victoria, downtown Vancouver, East Vancouver, North Vancouver and New Westminster. These offices usually received the largest allotment of plates, and it required an Oakalla Prison guard along with two or three inmate "trustees" to accomplish the task of restacking the boxes in the proper numerical order at each office. According to former MVB employee Ron Marston, staff at these regional offices would "chip in and give [the trustees] each a pack of 'tailor-made' cigarettes to show our appreciation of the accuracy of the job they did." However, before these plates could be issued, every box had to be opened and each plate checked before they were placed at the wickets for sale. As Marston recalls,

Some of those inmates just loved to place notes in between the plates if they knew what area they were going to on the distribution and let loose a tirade against the judge, or whoever they had a bone to pick or purposely juggle a

★ Fortunately, the 1949 plates did not experience any defects. Following the use of almost all available letter prefixes in 1948, the MVB determined that such a system could no longer cope with the number of vehicles being registered in the province and decided to return to an all-numeric serial for 1949. To accommodate this, and as had been done in the early 1930s, the MVB would utilize two different sizes of plates in 1949: a short version for five-digit serials and a longer version for six digits. This was likely a cost-saving measure as Superintendent George Hood had previously been on record opposing six-digit plates as they would have required an additional 31.5 tons of steel.[23]

TB Vets and the Evolution of the Keytag

In 1946, the Tuberculosis & Chest Disabled Veterans' Association (TB Vets) of British Columbia undertook the "small-scale" manufacturing of BC licence plates for drivers. The TB Vets plates, however, were intended for key chains and acted as identification tags that would guarantee the return of any lost keys. Based on the popular Disabled American Veterans (DAV) program in the United States, the funds raised by donations from motorists helped provide employment for returning veterans and aided others with basic necessities including groceries, clothing, transportation and even funeral costs.[24]

Popular with motorists, by the early 1970s the keytags were also sought after by thieves, who would find lost keys in a parking lot and use the licence plate number on the tag to track down the parked vehicle. Worse yet, if there were house keys on the ring, the thief could simply look up the victim's address on the registration papers in the car and loot the owner's home.

Along with the switch to renewable licence plates in 1970 (which introduced the potential for keytags to be valid over multiple years, thereby reducing the funds raised), the Vets moved away from actual licence plate numbers to a generic code in 1976.[25] In 2005, after almost 60 years of use, the licence plate design was abandoned in favour of images that would appeal to a broader audience.

★ Two veterans stamping licence plate numbers on miniature key chain tags to be distributed by the TB Vets in 1951 (far left).
ART JONES PHOTO, VANCOUVER PUBLIC LIBRARY 81605

few numbers. In one instance, I checked the top plate and it was what it was supposed to be, but when I turned the pair over there was C-FUN [a Vancouver top-40 radio station] stamped on the next pair. As you can tell from that, we did not stand around with nothing to do in the lean winter months at the tail end of the year.[26]

★ **"BCAA gets new licence plates"** The Penticton office of the BCAA displays the 1964 licence plates received from the MVB. PHOTO BY JACK STOCKS, COURTESY OKANAGAN ARCHIVE TRUST SOCIETY WWW.OLDPHOTOS.CA

★ A rare example of an error plate in which the J has been stamped upside down.

★ The elusive four-leaf clover of licence plates! Debra Chow, insurance manager at Jack W. Chow Insurance Ltd., displaying "Three of a Kind" passenger licence plates in 1996. The plates were discovered within a box of new, unissued plates. The mistake was attributed to a flaw in the set of plates numbered CBP-804 that resulted in one of these plates being destroyed and inadvertently replaced with an additional CBP-805. As a result, the box contained only one CBP-804, but three plates numbered CBP-805. Human error was the likely culprit in this case.[28]

JACK W. CHOW INSURANCE LTD.

In the mid-1970s, the MVB found itself trying to staff the Plate Shop at Oakalla without the benefit of inmate labour. Previously, all inmates doing time at Oakalla were serving sentences of no more than two years less a day; criminals sentenced to two years or more of incarceration were sent to the federal penitentiary at New Westminster. Yet, according to Dave Barrett, who was a social worker at both Oakalla and Haney (another Lower Mainland correctional facility) before he went into politics, most of the occupational training programs being offered to Oakalla inmates lasted at least three years, which meant it was impossible for prisoners serving two-year sentences to complete them. Whoever had "done the planning [had] not thought about [these] things!" wrote Barrett in his memoirs. "The whole foundation of this 'modern prison' was farcical, but nobody wanted to talk about it."[28] Nobody, that was, until Barrett became premier in 1972 and enacted reforms that allowed convicted prisoners to be transferred to smaller regional facilities, better equipped to provide training programs. A by-product of this reform was that the inmates who remained at Oakalla were on remand and could not be put to work in the Plate Shop because they were still considered innocent by the legal system.[29]

For senior staff at the MVB, the only way the Plate Shop could be kept operating was to bring in outside contractors, but before this could be done, the Plate Shop had to be secured from those prisoners still being housed at Oakalla. Barbed wire was placed around the outside of the shop, while the internal entrances from the prison were closed off. To ensure the safety of the contractors using the equipment, the practice of tying the workers' hands to the levers of the licence plate press continued. The Plate Shop would continue to operate with the help of hired labour for a few more years until the new Minister of Transport, Jack Davis, declared that it was time for the government to exit the plate business and put the contract out for tender. The MVB reviewed a number of bids before awarding the contract to Acme Signalisation Inc., which committed to produce the licence plates at their facility in Montreal and deliver them to the MVB's warehouse at 70 percent of Oakalla's cost.[30]

The contract awarded to Acme was for three years, and when the contract went out for tender a second time, another company, Hi Signs of Edmonton, won the competition. When the contract was up for renewal a third time, the provincial government found that there was now a political benefit to returning production to British Columbia. Keen to promote jobs as well as home-grown industries after the recession and "Restraint" program of the early 1980s,[31] the Social Credit administration of Bill Bennett approached Astrographic Industries Ltd., a Surrey sign-making firm, about the upcoming licence plate contract. Astrographic had already been producing the registration decals used on BC licence plates for a couple of years and was considered to be a very innovative company. Bennett was looking for just such a firm, as a requirement of the next contract was a new licence plate design featuring a stylized provincial flag. In March 1984, prior to awarding the contract, the premier met with representatives of Astrographic. It was at this meeting that a design showcasing the "Spirit Flag" in the middle of the plate was devised.

Confident in their ability to produce the design—known as a "close registered graphic"—Anders Ahlgren of Astrographic stated that they could produce the plates at an additional cost of only 30 cents per pair.[32] After some deliberation, the multi-million-dollar contract was awarded to Astrographic.

An important stipulation of the contract was that the new plates needed to be ready by January of 1985 so that all of the old blue plates would be off the roads ahead of the opening of the World's Fair (Expo 86) in Vancouver. This gave Astrographic less than nine months to devise a manufacturing process and produce sufficient quantities of the new plates so that the 800 Autoplan agents throughout the province would have stock by the end of 1984. To help Astrographic, the government offered the equipment from the Plate Shop at Oakalla (which had been dormant since the late 1970s) at a cost of $50,000. Ahlgren set about obtaining the other necessary components, such as silkscreening equipment, ovens,

★ Called "Spirit of BC," "Spirit Flag" or simply the "Flag," this logo was the official symbol of the Government of British Columbia from the early 1980s until about 2005.

★ After being awarded the licence plate contract, Astrographic knocked down a dividing wall and expanded into an adjacent space that had been occupied by a Corvette specialty shop. The plate-manufacturing process would take up almost the entire floor area of the combined facility, as can be seen in the image at left (circa mid-1980s).
ASTROGRAPHIC INDUSTRIES LTD.

Beautiful British Columbia
LAA 044
JUL 86

★ The new flag licence plate series began at LAA-000, with rumours that the first plate in the series was issued to the lieutenant-governor and the remaining 99 sets to other dignitaries.

★ Above, Sharon Henderson displays the new design in September of 1984.

VANCOUVER PROVINCE

sheeting, paints and related materials. In a feat that few thought possible, Ahlgren also developed a computerized system to run the production line within three months of the contract being signed. Unfortunately, in the rush to meet these deadlines, Astrographic overspent on equipment and labour and ended up doing itself financial harm.[33]

The design of the new flag plate was unveiled to much fanfare in early September of 1984. Behind the scenes, however, bugs were wreaking havoc with the manufacturing process. The computerized system devised by Ahlgren had to be geared to the slowest part of the plate-making process: the 200-ton press. The press kept malfunctioning when the characters were punched into the metal plate because the computer wasn't properly synched, and as soon as it got ahead of or behind the press the whole system would jam. These problems resulted in a crucial deadline being missed. Due to a quirk in the British Columbia vehicle registration year, approximately 580,000 motorists (or one-third of all motorists in the province) were set to renew at the end of February 1985. By the end of March, or almost 12 months after the contract was signed, only 100,000 sets had been manufactured.

As problems continued to plague the manufacturing process, only 300,000 sets of plates were ready by early May 1985, after which the MVB refused to predict when the new series might be ready. It was not until August 1 that sufficient licence plates were on hand to allow for the first sets to be issued, but by this point production delays assured that the old white-on-blue plates would be seen on the roads throughout the busy summer months of Expo 86.

Along with the early production problems that plagued the flag plates, Astrographic was not making any money on the plate contract. To help offset some of the set-up costs, Astrographic approached the government for additional funding, which was provided by the Ministry of Transportation. This proved to be only a stopgap measure, and it was not long before the company required further assistance. Having previously committed to the agreed price in

The Oddest "Army" on the Continent

In the aftermath of the Japanese swift attacks on Pearl Harbor, Singapore and Hong Kong in December 1941, British Columbia's coastal defences no longer seemed sufficient to rebuff an invasion. In response to mounting public pressure, the federal government created the Pacific Coast Militia Rangers (PCMR) in 1942. The Rangers were comprised of men who lived in rural parts of the province and were ineligible to serve overseas due to age, disability or occupation. By 1943, there were 126 different companies along the coast and in the interior of the province. Few resources were available to outfit the Rangers, so they had to scrounge or make their own items, such as signalling equipment, homemade grenades and, in some cases, identifying licence plates for their vehicles. Reminiscent of some of the homemade plates that were used by motorists a generation earlier, the PCMR licences were made of various materials such as wood, canvas and metal with hand-painted letters as well as the number of the Ranger unit.[34]

★ "Distinctive identification plates were authorized for those who use privately owned automobiles for Ranger work. The plates helped publicize the corps throughout B.C." This picture (above left) appeared in *Ranger* magazine, and Company No. 118 was West Point Grey (which also included Vancouver South and Marpole). **CFB ESQUIMALT NAVAL & MILITARY MUSEUM**

★ The examples on the right show the different materials that were used by the Rangers to make licence plates for their vehicles. No. 71 is wood with a rather detailed paint job; No. 117 is canvas stapled to a piece of wood; No. 129 is a painted piece of steel. **CITY OF PENTICTON ARCHIVES (NO. 71)**

the premier's office, the MVB held the line and refused any further payments. It is ironic that Astrographic went bankrupt within three years of winning the licence plate contract,[35] seeing as it had obtained that contract as part of the government's plan to promote local industry.

Despite this setback, Astrographic emerged from bankruptcy and continued to manufacture British Columbia licence plates until 2002, when Waldale Manufacturing of Amherst, Nova Scotia, won the contract. George Piva, the president of Astrographic, claims that the loss of the contract with British Columbia, while traumatic at the time in terms of staff layoffs, has turned out to be one of the best things that could have happened to the company. The die had been cast (pardon the pun) with the first contract signed with the Province in 1984 and, thereafter, the company was never able to charge an appropriate amount for the plates. Licence plates became a low-margin business for Astrographic, and there was never sufficient money to reinvest in equipment or adequately compensate staff. Although Astrographic continues to produce licence plates for Yukon Territory, it is now focused on the graphics side of the business (screen printing, signs, etc.), which has proven to be far more lucrative.[36]

Waldale, which won the BC contract in 2002, was subsequently acquired by the large German multinational Utsch. Controversy erupted in 2010 when Waldale-Utsch won the bid to supply Saskatchewan licence plates over the Regina firm Signal Industries (which had been manufacturing that province's plates since 1971).[37] As part of the contract, Waldale-Utsch is required to undertake "Saskatchewan hiring," and steps are being taken to open a production facility in that province.[38] It is likely that in the not-too-distant future, BC licence plates will be made in the "Land of Living Skies" instead of "Canada's Ocean Playground." Maybe one day they will even be made in "Beautiful British Columbia" again.

3 "JUMBLED FREAK"

On his way to open the 2010 Winter Olympic Games, Prime Minister Stephen Harper made a detour to Victoria to address the provincial legislature. After extolling the rugged beauty of the BC landscape and the various virtues of the people who call the province home, the prime minister waded into a simmering controversy. In pointing out that "Canadians from coast to coast to coast have known you for decades by the slogan on your licence plates—'Beautiful British Columbia,'" the prime minister appeared to be suggesting that maybe the province was not actually "The Best Place on Earth."[1] A favourite of Premier Gordon Campbell, "The Best Place on Earth" slogan first appeared in a series of tourism commercials released in 2004 before spreading to the masthead of all government communications. The decision to include the slogan on Olympic licence plates proved to be particularly polarizing; critics called it narcissistic, presumptuous, "embarrassingly arrogant," "egotistical," "shockingly pretentious" and "ignorant."[2] It also spawned an online petition, Facebook groups and endless blog and editorial rants. This episode demonstrates that, even for something as seemingly unimportant as

★ Premier Gordon Campbell (right) and VANOC CEO John Furlong (left) unveil the new BC licence plate celebrating the 2010 Olympic and Paralympic Winter Games and proclaiming British Columbia to be "The Best Place on Earth" at the head offices of ICBC on April 16, 2007.
JEFF VINNICK

a licence plate, a change in slogans or designs should be approached with extreme caution. While it is easy to mistake the design of licence plates as a simple marketing ploy or, on rare occasions, as public art, over time a licence plate can also represent common perceptions of identity—perceptions that, once forged, are not easily recast.[3] Many states and provinces have learned this lesson the hard way, with British Columbia's own experience mirroring the broader trend.

When motorists were first required to display licence plates in 1904, little thought was given to design. When the Province assumed responsibility for issuing licence plates in 1913, the legislation required that new licence plates be issued each year and that the Superintendent of Provincial Police pick which colours would be used. In an era when very few people owned an automobile, and the road network in British Columbia and neighbouring jurisdictions was poor, the idea that licence plates could be used as a promotional tool was inconceivable. This slowly began to change as various states and provinces started fighting counterfeiters by incorporating difficult-to-replicate designs. In 1910, Pennsylvania was the first to use a symbol when it introduced a validation tab in the shape of its signature "Keystone State" emblem. That same year Michigan incorporated the state seal, while California would use a bear emblem (taken from its state flag) to validate its licence plates in 1916.[4] Following Michigan's lead, a number of Canadian provinces included their coat of arms on their licence plates, including British Columbia from 1915 to 1917. Unfortunately, when viewed from any sort of distance, these official emblems became virtually indecipherable.

The year before British Columbia stopped using the coat of arms on its licence plates, Arizona included the profile of a Hereford steer in an attempt to support its cattle industry and boost sales. This simple yet transformative idea would change the face of licence plates across North America.

Within a decade, Idaho began stamping the shape of a potato into its plates, Utah issued a red plate designed to evoke images of its red-rock deserts, Kansas was purported to be considering an ear-of-corn design, while Massachusetts was embroiled in one of the first licence plate design controversies. On its 1928 licence plate, Massachusetts incorporated a codfish emblem that appeared to be swimming away from the name of the state and was subsequently blamed by local fishermen for causing one of the worst seasons in that industry's history. The State Registrar of Motor Vehicles tried to rectify this on the 1929 licence plate, with the codfish pictured swimming back to the state's name, but was only able to do so on a small block of plates.[5] One of the odder slogans adopted in this period was South Carolina's self-promotion as the "Iodine State"—a reference to the wonder element that was, at the time, considered an effective treatment for "idiocy."[6]

★ In this image of a 1915 BC licence plate, the coat of arms is barely legible.

IMAGE G-04986 COURTESY OF ROYAL BC MUSEUM, BC ARCHIVES

The reports from these states that made their way to British Columbia suggested that this form of advertising was inexpensive and "very successful in the results obtained." Not wanting to miss an opportunity to promote BC in similar ways, the Victoria Junior Chamber of Commerce suggested that the province's 1930 licence plates be manufactured in the shape of a wood log to serve as a travelling advertisement for the province's forestry industry. Although Attorney General R.H. Pooley claimed to support the idea at the time, the initiative was never acted upon.[7] Working against the log design was the impending transfer of production to Oakalla as the province attempted to rein in public expenses. Upgrading the equipment from J.R. Tacey & Son in order to produce a uniquely shaped licence plate was probably not high on the list of governmental priorities. It also did not help that the MVB pursued, over

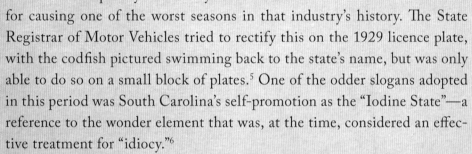

★ 1923 was the last year that the acronym "BC" would appear on British Columbia licence plates.

many decades, a policy to limit what it considered to be the unnecessary clutter adorning the licence plates issued by other jurisdictions.

One of the few exceptions to this clutter policy had occurred in the mid-1920s as the North American road network became more extensive, and motorists were increasingly able to travel long distances in their automobiles. Many states and provinces began to realize that the acronyms used to identify their licence plates were not always recognizable in other jurisdictions, and it became increasingly common for the full name of the issuing jurisdiction to be displayed on the licence plate.

Also working against a unique design such as a tree or a log was the fact that provincial policy was focused on thwarting forgers and ensuring that British Columbians continued to register their vehicles during the economic turmoil

★ Italicized fonts are very rare on a licence plate. The number of jurisdictions that have opted for them can be counted on the fingers of one hand. British Columbia used these dies between 1936 and 1954.[8]

of the 1930s. Consequently, the only design changes that occurred during this decade were unusual dies used for stamping out the characters.

With Canada officially at war as of September 1939, materials for licence plate production were rationed, and the chance for an elaborate new design diminished. Yet many in the business community continued to believe in the merits of using licence plates to promote tourism. As life returned to normal in 1948, the British Columbia Automobile Association (BCAA) resurrected a Thunderbird design, which had originally been proposed in 1940. The *Vancouver Province* newspaper also began to champion the cause, suggesting that a distinctive emblem, "such as a totem pole," as well as a slogan could be used to promote the province. The following year, the newspaper renewed its call for a slogan or emblem, noting that Wyoming used a bucking bronco, and a pelican adorned Louisiana's plates, while New Mexico proclaimed itself "The Land of Enchantment." Why, it asked, could "a little green fir tree or a totem pole [not] dress up B.C. licence plates and give us some advertising on the highways south of the line"?[9]

This question took on added urgency when it was revealed that Canadian tourists had, for the first time in 1950, spent more money in the United States than American tourists had spent in Canada. Local industry leaders determined that British Columbia needed to differentiate itself, namely through the commodification of West Coast Native culture. A group of "tourist conscious men" set about forming the Totem-Land Society in the belief that the totem pole, if properly marketed, could be used to lure tourists seeking a distinctive experience in British Columbia. With little input from local First Nations, the organization advocated for the use of the totem pole theme on such important items as letterheads, envelopes, invoices, shipping labels and licence plates.[10]

The Totem-Land Society emerged around the same time as the MVB commissioned the American consulting firm of Stevenson & Kellogg to undertake an "efficiency survey" of its operations. The MVB was struggling to cope

✴ Incorporating the outline of a state was popular throughout the 1940s and 1950s, with Tennessee, Pennsylvania and Montana, among others, employing this design. The 1950 Montana plate is particularly interesting as it also includes the slogan "The Treasure State" and an embossed statement at the bottom of the plate reminding motorists that the plate was "Prison Made."

with the skyrocketing demand for automobiles following the Second World War. Between 1945 and 1950, motor vehicle registrations in the province had doubled to almost 200,000.[11] The MVB, which historically had struggled to deal with the year-end renewal rush during the last week of February, now found itself totally overwhelmed. One of Stevenson & Kellogg's recommendations was to stagger the expiration of driver's licences to the holder's birthday in order to spread renewals more evenly across the calendar year. They also recommended that driver's licences be valid for five years, and that this coincide with the introduction of a new licence plate that could be renewed, through the use of validation tabs, for a similar five-year period.

These changes would not only result in greater administrative efficiency, but would also reduce the capital costs incurred by the Province in the manufacturing of licence plates. Prior to the outbreak of the Korean War in 1950, the price of steel had risen, which meant that the cost to produce that year's licence plates rose by $80,000. The use of renewal tabs was projected to moderate the impact of cyclical steel markets and make it easier to forecast production costs.

To accommodate multi-year licence plates, the Province announced that a new design would be used as well as a new "heavy-duty" material capable of withstanding five years of continuous use. Sensing an opportunity, members of the Totem-Land Society, reporters at the *Province* and other prominent Vancouverites began to lobby for the inclusion of a totem pole design and "Totem Land" slogan on the new licence plate. The absence of a slogan, these advocates claimed, was hurting BC tourism. Even Saskatchewan was better known in the United States, arguably because that province's licence plates proclaimed it to be "The Wheat Province." As "Totem Land" was not to everyone's liking, other slogans—from "Canada's Dogwood Province" and "The Pacific Province" to "Where the Big Salmon Jump," "Canada's Evergreen Playground" and the rather simple "Canada" (as it was feared that few Americans knew where British Columbia actually was)—were soon being suggested. Despite its anti-clutter policy, the MVB eventually relented to allow a Thunderbird figure to appear on the 1952 plates, but "Totem Land," or any other slogan, was deemed impractical.[12]

The Thunderbird left only enough space for a five-digit serial—despite vehicle registrations having reached 213,000 in 1951. To compensate, an unfamiliar alpha-numeric system was introduced to ensure enough combinations would be available to accommodate the anticipated 350,000 to 400,000 passenger vehicles that would be registered over the life of the plate.

The Thunderbird design was criticized almost immediately after its unveiling. The *Victoria Daily Colonist* questioned the relevance of totem poles to contemporary British Columbia ("How many genuine Indian carvings are left . . . to see?") and the merits of the design ("It isn't simple enough to be really striking"). Even the *Province* acknowledged the shortcomings of the design and editorialized that "the totem pole should look like a totem pole." One motorist, vacationing in Palm Springs, attempted to explain the design to his neighbours. After numerous attempts he concluded that "this mess of tin failed to create any degree of impression on my audience as to its worth-whileness and my explanation of the historic background and significance of the two emblems, although interesting to my listeners, could not be deciphered by them in that ill-conceived freak of metal." Even a founding member of the Totem-Land Society, John Post, proclaimed his disgust with the design:

> It doesn't look like anything. The totem is not even a copy of an original and is practically obliterated on the maple leaf background. All that was needed was a bright totem pole and the word "Totem–Land" or better still, "Land of the Totem" . . . we are making a mess of a colourful and interesting publicity idea for B.C.[13]

Other problems than merely the aesthetic began to plague the Thunderbird as it entered its second year of use in 1953. It was becoming apparent that

★ The 1952 licence plate design incorporating a Thunderbird totem pole inside the outline of a maple leaf was unveiled in September of 1951.

the aluminum base was deteriorating too quickly, and the renewal tabs had become an easy target for thieves. By March of 1953, a mere 14 months after the introduction of the totem plate, the government launched a study to assess the viability of its continued use. All signs pointed towards cancellation, and that August the attorney general decided to discontinue the plates following the 1954 registration year. In the end, the five-year experiment barely lasted a year and a half, leaving the MVB with over 1,000 pounds of scrap aluminum to dispose of. Although the Thunderbird plate was dead, the Totem-Land Society would continue to carry the torch and make overtures to the MVB to reinstate the emblem, or to try other designs such as a dogwood (the provincial flower) or a fish.[14] All of these were deemed unfeasible after 1955, when licence plate dimensions across North America were standardized, leaving limited space for elaborate designs.

Upset by the Province's decision to remove the Thunderbird, representatives of the Vancouver tourism industry were unfairly scathing in their assessment of the 1955 plate design. At a meeting of the Vancouver Tourist Association in early January of that year, the plates were variously described as "disagreeable," "ill-advised," "objectionable," "perfectly horrible," "featureless" and "uninspired." R. Rowe Holland, a director of the association, advised his fellow members that "the colour and appearance . . . makes a man ashamed to put them on his car."[15]

However, motorists and even the BCAA were generally untroubled. In defending the 1955 design, the MVB explained that one of the challenges it faced each year was settling on colours that would not clash with those of a neighbouring jurisdiction. It was an unwritten rule among issuing authorities at this time that no two adjoining jurisdictions should ever issue the same colour combination in the same registration year. The MVB maintained contact with the issuing authorities in Alberta, Yukon, Washington, Idaho and elsewhere in the region so that they had "a pretty good idea what the other fellow is going to do" in terms of colour combinations.[16]

After the reception given the 1955 plates, more conservative colour options were presented for the 1957 licence plates. Somehow, the lines of communication between Alberta and British Columbia broke down and both provinces ended up using a similar blue-on-white combination in 1957. MVB officials were apparently in some "anguish" over the mix-up.[17]

Colour problems continued to beset British Columbia licence plates in 1958 as the province utilized a symbolic green-and-gold scheme to commemorate the founding of the Crown Colony of British Columbia a century earlier. Green was in recognition of the province's forests (which also powered the economy), while the background colour was a tribute to the Fraser Canyon Gold Rush of 1858. Within days of the plate's release, complaints began to pour in as police officers felt the green did not present enough of a contrast against the gold background and made the registration numbers very difficult to read. The *Victoria Colonist* once again piled on, editorializing that "one is left wondering how on earth the authorities came to select such an unsuitable combination of colors."[18]

★ One of the concerns with the similar colour scheme used by Alberta and British Columbia in 1957 was that, when viewed at a distance, or on a vehicle with a low number, there might be some confusion as to which province had issued the plate. Use of the blue-on-white colour scheme marked the first time since 1941 that this combination had been used.

★ As was custom, the MVB experimented with various colour schemes 18 to 24 months before the issuance of the licence plates. The example pictured here shows the green-and-gold colour scheme that was ultimately selected for the 1958 licence plates and how it appeared on the 1956 base when being considered. The colour scheme was criticized as resembling "weak pea soup."[19]

Despite the annual complaint about colours, the tourism industry considered the 1958 plate series a "major victory" because for the first time the plates contained a slogan. That year marked the province's 100-year anniversary, and the provincial government had created a Centennial Committee to manage the party. In November of 1955, the committee paid a visit to the Golden Jubilee

committees overseeing similar celebrations in Alberta and Saskatchewan.[20] On returning to Victoria, the chair of the BC committee, Lawrie Wallace, worked with the attorney general and Superintendent of the MVB to ensure BC's 1958 licence plates bore the word "Centenary" and the date of 1858.

★ The 1955 Saskatchewan licence plate, which commemorated the province's Golden Jubilee, served as the template for the 1958 BC licence plate.

Decoding Licence Plate Colours

In an era before computer-applied graphic images, the colour scheme employed on a licence plate carried symbolic value.

It was quite common for certain American states to adopt the school colours of the local college or university on their licence plates. In the southern US, where football is king, the university colours often symbolized an important bowl win. The 1951 Tennessee plates, for example, sport the colours of the University of Tennessee, which beat the University of Texas in the 1951 Cotton Bowl. In 1963, the State of Illinois issued licence plates in the corporate colours of John Deere to commemorate the 125th anniversary of the company, which is headquartered in Moline, Illinois.

The orange-on-turquoise colour scheme used on the 1938 Ontario licence plates was at the behest of the Minister of Highways, who was a member of the True Blue and Orange Lodge.[21] When Manitoba decided to issue a new licence plate in 1983, the colours were purportedly going to be red and blue on white, which happened to coincide with the colours of the governing Conservative Party. After the 1981 provincial election, the colours of the plates "mysteriously" became red and black on white, the colours of the newly elected New Democratic Party.

After the 1957 colour conflict between Alberta and BC, the MVB delegated the selection of the 1959 colour scheme to its paint contractor, the British America Paint Company. BAPCO's only criteria were to provide durability and uniqueness of colour, ensuring that BC licence plates did not portray the same "dead colours" that had raised the wrath of the Vancouver tourism industry in the mid-1950s and that they did not conflict with a neighbouring state or province. The result was a vivid pastel combination of turquoise on maroon, which was reversed for the 1960 series. The 1961 and 1962 series were equally striking, with a pink-and-maroon colour scheme that garnered BC the distinction of having the most exotic plates in North America according to the American Automobile Association (AAA). The local reaction was more mixed, with one newspaper declaring the 1961 colour scheme "ghastly, frightful, unprintably awful, and an appalling offence to the sensibilities." Another commented that the colour combination has "never been a hit with the motoring public . . . [and] the effect was considered pretty awful."[22]

Having run the gamut of dead, conflicting, illegible and wildly flamboyant colour schemes, the MVB reverted to a more "rational" blue-and-white scheme in 1963. Following its introduction, Minister of Recreation and Conservation Earle Westwood suggested the colours be made permanent as they were the same as those used on the BC Toll Authority ferries.[23] British Columbia has followed this prescription of alternating blue-and-white colour schemes on passenger licence plates ever since. Following the success of the centennial slogan, proposals for other slogans continued to percolate. One promoted BC as a "sportsman's paradise" in 1959, but it was rejected because it was thought to "appeal to only 10 per cent of the tourists." The Prince George Board of Trade thought a more inclusive slogan might be "Opportunities Unlimited," while the Totem-Land Society predictably

★ Some of the wildest colours ever seen on licence plates appeared in BC between 1959 and 1962.

★ CITY OF VANCOUVER ARCHIVES, AM1517-S1, LESLIE SHERATON

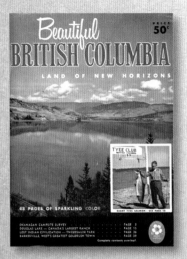

suggested "Totem Land." Momentum for the word "Beautiful" began to build after the Department of Tourism initiated a marketing program in 1959 that included the publication of a magazine called *Beautiful British Columbia*, which was designed to showcase the province within Canada and around the world. When it was formally announced that the "Beautiful" slogan would appear on provincial licence plates in 1964, the MVB was forced to respond to critics by clarifying that the plates were simply stating the truth and not trying to sell any magazines. The Totem-Land Society registered its disdain for the slogan by claiming "Beautiful" was too general and not exclusively symbolic of British Columbia, while the *Province* felt the term was "too platitudinous."[24] Coincidentally, the Quebec government had introduced "La Belle Province" slogan in 1963.

In the mid-1960s, another centennial committee was formed, this time by the federal government in Ottawa, to mark the 100th anniversary of Canadian Confederation. The National Centennial Commission began contacting each of the provinces to see if they would be interested in having their 1967 licence plates carry either an emblem or slogan commemorating the anniversary.[25] A popular misconception has arisen over the years that the commission succeeded in convincing only five provinces to mark the occasion on their licence plates. Less well known is the fact that British Columbia made what would be the only exception to its policy on licence plate colours in 1967 by allowing the passenger series to be red and white—a reflection of the national colours (proclaimed in 1921 and incorporated in the new national flag in 1965).[26]

Shortly before the release of the 1967 Canadian Centennial plate, the MVB began to explore alternatives to the all-numeric serial as vehicle registrations neared the one million mark and exhaustion of the six-digit format. Minister of Recreation and Conservation William K. Kiernan publicly advocated for letter prefixes to show which part of the province a vehicle was from. He felt this would aid in determining how much inter-regional travel was occurring within the province. The MVB was

Don't Hate Us Because We're Beautiful

While it is popularly assumed that Quebec's adoption of the "Je me souviens" ("I remember") slogan in 1978 reflected separatist undertones, I have always wondered if the slogan is not aimed squarely at British Columbians and our pretension to be "Beautiful." In the overweening language of licence plate slogans, are Quebecers saying they will always remember who was beautiful first?

In all seriousness, it has been argued that the political motivations behind the switch were that by removing "La Belle Province," the Parti Québécois officials were removing any provincial connotation from the licence plates, suggesting that Quebec may not be a Canadian province in the future. Second, the new phrase, "Je me souviens," "evokes for Quebec nationalists the three centuries of French presence in North America."

Others have challenged British Columbia in its assertion of beauty. In the mid-1980s, Utah held a contest to pick a new licence plate slogan and came awfully close to choosing the peculiarly crafted "beeUTAHful" (which makes more sense if you know that the honeybee is the official state insect). Utah ultimately opted for the more provocative, but clearly misplaced, claim to possess the "Greatest Snow on Earth" (a slogan chosen to boost the state's chances of landing the 1992 Winter Olympic Games).

To set the record straight, BC would roll out a similar slogan on its own Olympic licence plates 20 years later, boldly proclaiming itself "The Best Place on Earth"! Not to be outdone, New Mexico, tongue in cheek, branded itself "The Best Place in the Universe" shortly thereafter.[27]

"The Beautiful Province" (1963)   "Beautiful British Columbia" (1964)   Quebec - "I Remember" (1978)

less convinced, as many plates were issued by mail, and around 20 percent of drivers changed their address in a given year.[28] It was also very important that no offensive combinations be issued, as the plates would be "advertising for the Province," and it would not reflect well if the first three letters of the plates spelled out something obnoxious. California helped out by providing its own list of potentially offensive combinations, to which the MVB added a few more (such as CBC, CCF and NDP).[29]

California had already tackled the issue of offensive letter combinations when it switched to the "AAA" format. The state engaged the services of a professor at the linguistics department at UC Berkeley to screen out all unsuitable words. This list was shared with the MVB, which added its own Canadian elements. One particular combination—HBC—resulted in long lineups forming at the Richmond MVB office. Staff of the Hudson's Bay Company had found out where these plates were being issued and sought them out for their personal vehicles.[30]

Only as printing technology improved and the cost of using multiple colours and graphics on licence plates became more feasible did the government begin to explore alternatives to the static blue-and-white designs that had appeared throughout the 1970s. Of the designs that were explored (see bottom left of this page), most depicted the rugged geography of the province, or the dogwood (the provincial flower), as well as an alternative slogan—"Super, Natural"—which was a favourite of the then-governing Social Credit Party under Premier Bill Bennett.

Although these designs were never adopted, they generally conformed to the belief that a licence plate should promote some aspect of a local economy or tourism. As was seen with the changing of slogans in Quebec a few years earlier, this model was beginning to transform as some governments were using their licence plates for overt political purposes, such as promoting a nationalist identity and ideology. In 1971, New Hampshire replaced its "Scenic" slogan with the state's motto "Live Free or Die"; the following year New Brunswick retired its "Picture Province" slogan (in use since 1958) in favour of the bilingual-friendly spelling of the province's name in English and French.[31] British Columbia was not immune to this trend, as the re-election of the Social Credit Party in 1983 would lead to a massive political rebranding of the provincial government. In the lead-up to the election, Bennett transformed his party from a largely volunteer outfit to a professional party machine by bringing in outside experts. According to Bob Plecas, a deputy minister in Bennett's administration,

> One of [the experts'] *first projects was to design a new licence plate for the province incorporating the "wavey flag" symbol that had been used extensively by the Social Credit Party in its election campaigns. Make the people think there is no difference between Social Credit and the government. When brought to cabinet for final approval, Bennett remarked: "I can hardly wait to see [Opposition leader] Dave Barrett fasten this licence plate to his car."[32]*

An important condition of the licence plate contract that the government had awarded to Astrographic in March of 1984, and which Bennett himself had insisted upon, was a commitment to incorporate the "wavey flag."[33] Bennett had wanted the new plate series ready for issuance by January of 1985 so that all vehicles in the province would be displaying the logo when the World Exposition opened in Vancouver on May 2, 1986. Production problems delayed the unveiling until March, when Bennett symbolically awarded the "first" licence plate in the series—EXPO 86—to Rick Hansen as he set off on his Man in Motion World Tour from the Oakridge Shopping Centre in Vancouver. Distribution of the new plate series would not occur until August 1985, meaning some of the old blue plates issued in 1979 were still seen on the roads throughout the first three months of Expo.

★ When Tom Wayman defaced the Expo 86 logo that adorned the renewal decals that year, he was charged by police.[34]

VANCOUVER PROVINCE

★ In truth, the "first" licence plate from the new series—EXPO 86—was anything but. It was actually a personalized licence plate that had been produced using the new "wavey flag" design. The true first plate from the new series was LAA-001, which was reported to have been issued to Lieutenant-Governor Robert Rogers. The alpha-numerical equivalent of Hansen's plate—EXP-086—would have been issued in 1998.

RICK HANSEN FOUNDATION

★ Could this have been Dave Barrett's licence plate? We may never know, but whoever had this plate was clearly opposed to the Social Credit government's attempt to use the new plates to promote itself.

One of the great ironies regarding the push to have the new flag design licence plates on the road ahead of the opening of Expo 86 was that when the gates to the fair finally opened, one of the main family attractions—the water park featuring UFO-H2O—proudly displayed an oversized representation of the old-style licence plate!

Given the latent political symbolism attached to the flag as an emblem of the Social Credit Party, the licence plate's longevity is a curious mystery. Following the election of a New Democratic Party administration in the early 1990s, Astrographic proposed a series of new designs that would have refocused the messaging back to tourism. The idea was to create a series of geography-themed licence plate designs representing different parts of the province, such as the Naramata Bench (an alluvial fan renowned for its orchards and vineyards) or the forests around Prince George. Astrographic also wanted to explore the emerging digital technology of "flat plates," a printing technique that eliminates the need for embossing and allows licence plates to be manufactured in a similar way to photographs. New York and Colorado were pioneering the use of this new technology, and Astrographic was quick to see its potential. Astrographic also wanted to move into specialty-themed licence plates, such as sports teams, as these would generate additional revenues for organizations and the provincial government. Unfortunately, according to George Piva of Astrographic, there are "always people that kill ideas."[35]

★ After Expo concluded, an auction was held and essentially everything associated with the fair was sold. While larger, more notable items—such as the hockey stick in Duncan—remain easy to identify, the fate of UFO-H2O remained a mystery. It turns out the green fellow was acquired by the Mount Layton Hot Springs Resort near Terrace. Time has not been kind to UFO-H2O, as it ceased being an active water park feature when its air and timing systems started to fail many years ago.
JON LASIUK

★ Pictured are some of the designs that could have replaced the flag designs in the early 1990s if a proposal by Astrographic had been implemented by ICBC.
ASTROGRAPHIC INDUSTRIES LTD.

Almost 25,000,000 pairs of flag licence plates have rolled off the Astrographic and Waldale presses over the past three decades, and a whole generation of British Columbians has been raised staring out their windshields at the symbol of a long-defunct political party.

ENDURING SLOGANS

SLOGAN	PROVINCE	YEARS IN USE
"Beautiful"	British Columbia	1964–present
"Canada's Ocean Playground"	Nova Scotia	1972–present
"Wild Rose Country"	Alberta	1973–present
Bilingual slogan (New / Nouveau)	New Brunswick	1972–2009
"Je me souviens"	Quebec	1978–present
"The Klondike"	Yukon	1978–present
"Yours to Discover"	Ontario	1982–present
"Friendly"	Manitoba	1983–present
"Explore Canada's Arctic"	NWT	1986–2010
"Land of the Midnight Sun"	Yukon	1953–1970

★ Pictured are some prototype designs that were created by Astrographic in the 1990s to demonstrate how organizations such as the University of British Columbia or the BC Children's Hospital Foundation could use licence plates as a fundraising mechanism.
ASTROGRAPHIC INDUSTRIES LTD.

As staid as the flag design has become over the past generation, the 000-AAA format is expected to run out of available combinations in 2014. The introduction of a new licence plate series is generally accompanied by a new design, and ICBC has already begun to show its hand with some of the new design features incorporated on the new consular and motorcycle bases. Unfortunately, the government has displayed a shocking absence of creativity or inspiration and is planning to simply swap out the flag logo for the "BC Mark" (which has been popular with the governing Liberal Party administration since 2005). ICBC has already announced that the new format being considered after plate No. 999-XXX is issued (in 2014), is AA0-00A,[36] which is a "second-best" option stemming from the limitations imposed by ICBC's computer system.

A Licence Plate Fit for a Princess

In 1951, Princess Elizabeth and the Duke of Edinburgh went on a tour of Canada to thank Canadians for their military support of the "mother country." A coast-to-coast tour was organized, and the Royals arrived in Vancouver on October 20. Although the tour was principally conducted by rail, for short distances within cities such as Vancouver and Victoria, the Royals travelled by car.

★ As with past royal tours, a number of different vehicles were used. In the photo at left, the princess and duke are seen leaving the Legislative Buildings in Victoria. Unfortunately, the special licence plate issued for this tour is obscured by bystanders, but it can be seen clearly at an early stop in the tour outside Thunder Bay, Ontario.

IMAGE B-06094 COURTESY OF ROYAL BC MUSEUM, BC ARCHIVES (FAR LEFT) AND THUNDER BAY PUBLIC LIBRARY (LEFT)

As the story goes, a GM dealership in Toronto was asked to prepare six cars to "dignitary standards of class and security" to be used as part of the tour, two of which would stay in the Toronto area, while the others would be shared between the Maritime and western provinces. At the conclusion of the royal visit, the cars were to be sent back to the General Motors plant in Detroit. The owner of the dealership had other ideas, envisioning the day he would give his daughter away in marriage and drive her to the ceremony in the same car used by a princess. So, one of the black convertible Cadillacs—as well as the special licence plates that accompanied it—were kept in anticipation of the wedding day. Less than four months after this tour, Princess Elizabeth would become queen following the death of her father, King George VI.

Almost 40 years later, the convertible Cadillac was long gone, but the family had kept the special licence plate as a souvenir. Seeking to fund a trip to New York City, the grandson of the dealership owner sold the plate to a local collector in 1989.[37]

★ The ceremonial handover? It is not clear what is taking place in this photo, but it is assumed to be the transferring of the keys to the vehicle. Clearly visible is the special royal licence plate—also pictured at left. This photo was taken in Victoria in October of 1951.

IMAGE I-02157 COURTESY OF ROYAL BC MUSEUM, BC ARCHIVES (FAR LEFT)

Ideally, ICBC should follow other states and provinces, such as California, Washington, Arizona, Texas and Alberta, and introduce a seven-digit format as this would allow for exponentially more combinations. Options could include a design competition or an online public survey to select from in-house designs that previously would have been presented only to the minister or cabinet for approval (such as occurred with the Veteran and Olympic designs). These ideas have been undertaken by numerous other jurisdictions and, when handled right, can help defuse or avoid the public outcry and controversy that may arise in response to an ill-conceived design or slogan.

★ Consul licence plates, which are used by the consular staff of foreign countries based in British Columbia, were redesigned in 2007 to be more consistent with consular plates issued in Ontario. "The Best Place on Earth" slogan was considered, but it was ultimately deemed to be poor form to require foreign representatives to display this on their vehicles.

★ A prototype that never made it beyond the design stage, this particular plate sought to incorporate the "BC Mark"— the official government emblem —and introduce "The Best Place on Earth" slogan onto a licence plate design.

The ROAD to a PERMANENT PLATE

4

When licence plates became standardized in 1913, motorists, much to their annoyance, now had to trudge outside each year in the dead of winter, unscrew rusty bolts and attach a new pair of plates to their cars—even though most expired plates were in good enough shape to endure a few more years of service.

With no other use, these expired plates were either discarded or nailed to the garage wall for posterity. The resources that went into producing annual licence plates—from the cost of procuring the necessary materials to paying for equipment and labour—eventually began to weigh on the provincial budget. From an estimated cost of $15,000 in 1930, the price of licence plate production increased to an estimated $300,000 in 1947. This led the Province to seek solutions that would not only reduce the cost to taxpayers, but also conserve valuable resources. The obvious solution was to allow licence plates to be used over multiple years—the return of a permanent plate. Getting there, however, proved to be an arduous task and one that would see the cost of licence plate manufacturing double to $600,000.[1]

The event that did the most to convince the Province to reintroduce the "permanent plate" was the commencement of the Second World War. In order

★ In this photo (above, left), Fred Jones is having his new 1935 No. 4 licence plate attached to his 1921–22 Packard at the local dealership in Victoria. The first person who was issued the No. 4 plate in 1904 was Dr. E.C. Hart, who brought the first car to Victoria two years earlier. Hart's claim to the number lapsed, and when the Province introduced standardized licence plates in 1913, the No. 4 was issued to Jones, who would retain the number into the 1950s. **COURTESY OF THE NATIONAL AUTOMOTIVE HISTORY COLLECTION, DETROIT PUBLIC LIBRARY**

★ Jones's collection was subsequently acquired by Len Garrison (above right), a Ladner-based collector, in the mid-1960s. Garrison would track down subsequent No. 4s issued through to 1969—thereby assembling one of the most impressive North American licence plate "runs" known to exist. **PIERRE DELACÔTE**

to conserve materials needed for the war effort, the federal government had advised the provinces to limit the amount of metal and paint going into licence plate production. In Manitoba, motorists were required to return their 1941 front plate in order to receive a set of 1942 plates; Quebec used a Masonite board in 1944; and Alberta issued a windshield sticker to validate registrations in 1945.

A number of US states were even more creative. Louisiana, for example, used bagasse, a fibre derived from sugar cane. One of the most popular stories among licence plate enthusiasts involves a hungry goat and a 1943 Illinois plate. Illinois had decided to utilize a fibreboard licence plate derived from soybeans to cope with material shortages. As is their wont, this particular goat nibbled

144-414
QUEBEC - 44

SASK. 1944
43298
PROVINCIAL TAX COMMISSION
HIGHWAY TRAFFIC BOARD

★ Shown above is an example of a 1944 Quebec licence plate made out of fibreboard, while the windshield decal shown below it was issued by Saskatchewan and allowed motorists in that province to continue to use their 1943 licence plates for another year.

★ Finding the same numbers for a 1942 and 1943 licence plate usually only occurs if the number is lower than 3,000, as the MVB allowed people to request the same numbers from this block each year. The matching plates shown above (No. 50-551) are quite rare and would have originally been manufactured as a pair for issuance in 1942.

★ This image is the back of the 1943 licence plate and has been reversed so that it is easier to discern the faint outline where the 2 in 42 was before being re-stamped to a 3.

at a plate that had recently been affixed to a vehicle and, deciding it was to his liking, proceeded to eat the entire offering. Back in British Columbia, and aware that regulations mandating the conservation of materials were coming, the MVB had already decided to split the licence plate sets produced for 1942, sending half of the run back to Oakalla to be re-stamped with a 1943 date and painted with new colours for the coming year.

In 1943, the federal government mandated that all provinces issue their licence plates as singles, a measure that would remain in effect until 1947. Producing a single licence plate, however, did not address the still-significant input of materials required or the discarding of perfectly good plates at the end of the year (although metal drives conducted in support of the war effort did manage to collect a fair number of these plates), and it did not alleviate the inconvenience to motorists of having to replace their plates each year. In response, the main organization representing the interests of motorists in the province, the British Columbia Automobile Association (BCAA), began to advocate for the use of windshield stickers as a more cost-effective way to register vehicles in 1943. BCAA considered stickers to be the superior option as they required fewer physical resources, were less expensive, could be easily affixed to the inside of a windshield and would allow motorists to continue using their licence plates over multiple years.[2]

Windshield stickers had actually been used 10 years earlier when the Tolmie administration had gifted motorists two free months of registration in 1933 in an effort to stem the flood of vehicles being taken off the road during the Great Depression. Declining vehicle use was detrimental to small businesses that had become reliant on trucks and cars for the delivery of goods, as well as to the gas stations and mechanics that serviced these vehicles. This offer was repeated again in 1934 after the government announced it was changing the annual licensing year from a calendar year to a year ending on the last day of February.[3]

When restrictions were eased after the war, the MVB announced that it would once again issue front and rear licence plates starting in 1948. Doing so would require thousands of tons of additional steel each year, at a cost of approximately $300,000. No doubt reflecting the thoughts of their readers, both the *Daily Colonist* and *Province* encouraged the MVB to consider a permanent plate similar to the one that had just been introduced in Manitoba, but which could be renewed through the use of windshield stickers. The pressure on the MVB mounted when Washington announced that its 1947 licence plates would be used for an initial two-year period, and, if that proved successful, for a further five years. This would save the state approximately $200,000 a year. The MVB remained skeptical of permanent plates, however, as a notable number of motorists had attempted to take advantage of the two bonus months of registration in 1933 and 1934 by simply placing a square piece of white paper in their windshield, mimicking the official sticker. Moreover, a metal renewal tab was easier to counterfeit than a set of licence plates, and the accounting system needed to administer such a renewal scheme was so cumbersome that it would offset any financial savings associated with a permanent plate.[4]

Events beyond the MVB's control, however, would soon force it to reconsider its position. As soldiers demobilized and returned home from the war, vehicle registrations in the province increased by 70 percent, from 132,282 to 225,327 for the five-year period between 1945 and 1949.[5] The Stevenson & Kellogg report had already confirmed that substantial savings could be realized if the MVB introduced a renewable licence plate.[6]

The fine for drivers who didn't obtain the proper registration increased under the new system from 10 to 25 dollars. Overjoyed at the prospect of permanent plates, the *Province* ran an editorial blowing its own horn:

Poppies Bloom on BC Plates

Many US states have a long tradition of issuing special optional licence plates to veterans who have served in various military campaigns. Seeing vehicles that sported these plates during trips to the US gave Colonel Archie Steacy, now retired, of North Vancouver the idea that British Columbia should recognize its veterans in a similar way prior to the 60th anniversary of the D-Day landing in Normandy on June 6, 2004. As president of the British Columbia Veterans Commemorative Association (BCVCA), Steacy, along with Sharel Fraser of Veterans Affairs, arranged a meeting with Premier Gordon Campbell and Solicitor General Rich Coleman to discuss the idea in late 2003. By the end of the meeting, which lasted only 15 minutes, Campbell declared, "Archie, we're going to do it."

There would be only four months in which to hammer out all the details, including the design of the licence plate, and a working group was quickly established. Everyone agreed that the plate should have a more striking design than the simple poppy and flag motifs that adorned other provincial veteran plates. Yet many of the initial proposals were deemed unsatisfactory—"some [were] quite conservative, and some [were] 'flower power' poppy images that looked like they dropped right out of the '60s." With only days before an important deadline and no design in place, one of the committee members contacted Veterans Affairs in Ottawa to ask if someone from their office would be able to head over to the National War Memorial and take some high-quality digital photos.

Unfortunately, the photos provided by Veterans Affairs did not turn out as expected. So another member of the design committee, Mary Kletchko, went on the Internet and found a striking image of the National War Memorial on a site maintained by Memorial University. This picture was duly commandeered for the task at hand, cropped, altered to extend the sky, overlaid with the obligatory poppy and Canadian flag and, voila, the now familiar Veteran licence plate was born.[7]

★ This design was not selected as it was considered to be "a bit too busy," and there was a concern that the soldiers would be obscured by the licence plate numbers, and vice versa. The powder-blue background of the actual Veteran plate design links the different eras of the Canadian military as represented by the War Memorial and more recent peacekeeping missions. COPYRIGHT ICBC, ALL RIGHTS RESERVED ★ Gordon Campbell and Archie Steacy at the unveiling of the British Columbia Veteran licence plate on June 2, 2004.

For two and a half years this newspaper has been after the Provincial Government to provide B.C. automobiles with permanent, heavy-duty licence plates and eliminate all the work and trouble of annual renewals. For a long time the government authorities took a dim view of the proposal and indicated they felt it impractical . . . The Province is glad it was able to do its bit in stirring the government into action, but regrets it takes officialdom so long to warm to new ideas.[8]

Stevenson & Kellogg's recommendations came too late to be fully incorporated for 1951 as the Plate Shop at Oakalla was already preparing to manufacture that year's series. As a compromise, a small quantity of plates would be made for new registrations, but the majority of motorists would be renewing their licence plates through the use of a renewal tab (or "strip") in 1951. This would allow the MVB to begin planning for the switch to a permanent plate in 1952. In a foreshadowing of future problems, not all motorists knew where they were supposed to attach the strips to their 1950 licence plates. Some placed the strips on top, which obscured their licence plate number and raised the ire of local police, who warned that failure to place these strips along the bottom of the licence plate would result in a ticket. Police also began to report back to the MVB that the serial number stamped on each of the strips was essentially invisible from a distance of more than a few feet, thereby making it virtually impossible to identify a stolen strip.[9]

Inexplicably, nothing was done to correct this problem on the Thunderbird plate, and within

★ Within two weeks of the MVB announcing that it was exploring the introduction of permanent plates, the *Province* ran a short story entitled "Local Man Invents Lightup Licence Plate." Vancouver resident Laurence Walshe (pictured at left) had come forward with an illuminated licence plate that he had invented (and patented) back in 1921 while living in Saskatchewan.

Although Walshe had not been able to convince any other province or state about the merits of his invention in the intervening 28 years, he proclaimed it could save BC precisely $219,132 over five years. The plate was designed to improve visibility at night by having a light illuminate the numbers, while a removable panel allowed for the year to be easily changed.[10] *VANCOUVER SUN*

★ The 1950 licence plate (below left) had not been intended for use over multiple years. As a result, the design of a renewal tab (or "strip") was somewhat awkward because there was no space to properly display the registration number, and the 1950 expiry date was clearly visible at the right-hand side of the plate.

★ Shown above is a late-issue Thunderbird plate (absent a Thunderbird), likely released in either 1953 or 1954, with examples of the '53 and '54 renewal tabs.

weeks of the 1953 renewal tabs being issued, reports began to circulate about a rash of thefts of the easy-to-remove tabs. The BCAA even went as far as to recommend that members have their tabs riveted onto their plates to frustrate potential thieves. By the middle of March, Attorney General Robert Bonner conceded that there were significant problems with the tabs and they might be discontinued. Alarmed, the *Victoria Times* editorialized that "permanent plates" had much in their favour, but Bonner announced that the renewal tab system would be abandoned after 1954. To limit the fallout from what was quickly shaping up as a government boondoggle, Bonner advised motorists that in "returning to steel plates and abandoning the tab system we can give [you] better service at less cost."[11]

The inexorable rise in vehicle registrations throughout North America continued into the 1950s and 1960s, and British Columbia was not alone in having to confront the cost of producing and distributing hundreds of thousands of licence plates each year. In 1953, Missouri became the first state to issue plastic decals to be applied directly to the previous year's licence plate (as opposed to the windshield). In Canada, Nova Scotia, New Brunswick and Prince Edward Island began to use similar plastic decals as early as 1963.

Always seeking to reduce costs, the Plate Shop at Oakalla began exploring the logistics of introducing plastic decals in the mid-1960s after British Columbia joined the Western Compact and began to issue plastic registration decals to inter-provincial commercial trucks. After the Thunderbird fiasco, one of the first things the Plate Shop did was to find a durable material that could withstand at least five years of continual use. Next, decals and a small cellophane envelope in which to place them were sourced at seven cents a set. Given that Oakalla could produce a pair of licence plates for 34 cents, the 1965 series of 650,000 passenger plates cost $221,000. If, however, decals had been used in 1965, the cost to renew every passenger vehicle in

MARILYN PECKHAM

LYNNE MILES

N KOVICH

DENNIS ROWE

ELLEN MONK

★ One of these kids is not like the others! The image of the 1957 licence plates being modelled by Dennis Rowe (left) is unique for obvious reasons, as well as the fact that the actual plates still exist. Shown above Dennis are Marilyn Peckham (1959), Karen Kovich (1967), Ellen Monk (1969) and Lynne Miles (1970). Unfortunately, the identity of the woman displaying the 1963 plate is unknown.

VANCOUVER PROVINCE PHOTO, VANCOUVER PUBLIC LIBRARY 41205, RAY ALLAN / *VANCOUVER SUN*,
IAN MCKAIN / *VICTORIA TIMES COLONIST*, DENI EAGLAND / *VANCOUVER SUN*, BILL DENNETT / *VANCOUVER SUN*

★ **THE FIRST MODERN BC DECALS**
Under the Western Compact, a commercial prorated licensing vehicle was required to display a prorate plate from its base jurisdiction as well as a "Bingo" plate, which displayed decals from other states and provinces the vehicle was registered to operate in. These particular decals (above) would have been issued to out-of-province commercial truck operators. "Power" refers to the power unit, which is also the main truck, while trailers in this period would have been issued different decals that featured the letters TRLR. **IAN SLADE**

the province would have amounted to no more than \$45,500.[12] Decals would also significantly reduce the total number of new plates required each year to accommodate new registrations. Consider that in 1969 (the final year that annual passenger licence plates were issued) there were 790,493 vehicles registered in British Columbia, and the MVB ordered 808,000 sets of plates. Over 40 years later, the number of registered vehicles has increased to over two million (2010), and, excluding those years in which a new base plate was issued—such as 1979 and 1985—the number of passenger plates ordered has rarely exceeded 600,000 sets.[13]

★ In the 1965 Commercial Truck series, approximately 5,000 to 6,000 plates display what appears to be a decal box at the bottom of the plate. While the reason for this decal box remains a mystery, the plates did appear at the same time that the Oakalla Plate Shop was investigating the feasibility of a permanent plate with a material that would allow licence plates to be used for an extended period of time (possibly even four years). When renewal decals were introduced in 1970, the design of the new licence plate looked very similar to the 1965 commercial plate variation.

While the Plate Shop was experimenting with materials and designs, the Motor Vehicle Branch began investigating a new serial format as vehicle registrations approached the one million mark. Interestingly, the MVB was forced to confirm that such a study was underway after Minister for Recreation and Conservation William Kenneth Kiernan attempted to pre-empt its findings by suggesting that BC licence plates would be geographically coded by letter prefixes in order to better track internal tourist traffic.[14] The task of investigating a new format fell to Ron Marston, who managed the MVB's audit section at the time. Marston recalls being handed a very thick file containing six different

Plates on Parade In 1966, as the Province began to gear up for the celebration of the 100th anniversary of the merger between the Crown Colonies of Vancouver Island and British Columbia, and the Canadian Centennial the following year, Attorney General Robert Bonner announced the creation of a new antique vehicle licence plate. Bonner felt that many of the public events that would be held over the next two years would be enlivened by the participation of vintage cars. As these older vehicles were not generally used on a daily basis, it did not make sense for their owners to take out an annual registration.

Consequently, the Antique plates became the first permanent licence plates issued by the MVB as they would be good for the life of the vehicle and never needed to be replaced. At the time of their release, Bonner felt compelled to state that the licence plates were not meant to denote the Liquor Control Board, a misconception that was attributed to the word "Vintage" displayed at the top of the plate.

Twenty-four years later, the Province introduced a new Collector licence plate, which allowed for greater flexibility than the Antique plates by permitting a vehicle to be operated for pleasure use. As a result, Collector plates have become far more popular than Antique plates with vintage car owners—approximately 43,000 Collector plates have been issued since 1990, compared with 8,300 Antique plates since 1966.[15]

★ Attorney General Robert Bonner displays an example of the Antique licence plates that he had announced on February 18, 1966. **JIM RYAN**

★ The 1970 decal served no purpose other than to provide motorists with practice in how to apply a registration decal to a licence plate.

Accordingly, the decal is unique in that it is the only one to have been issued without a serial number for accounting purposes.

plate configurations, including the AAA-000 format that had been introduced by California in 1956, and being instructed to figure out which one would work best in British Columbia. One of the limiting factors that had to be considered was that the presses at Oakalla could only produce a licence plate with a maximum of six characters. Any combination of letters and numbers also had to be easily recognizable so that a witness to a vehicle incident could remember the licence plate number and recall it later for authorities. Marston recommended adopting the California system because of its simplicity and relative ease of administration. Precise details regarding the switch were only released in March of 1969. Motorists were advised that their next set of licence plates would be used for a trial period of three years. If this proved successful, these plates would be replaced by a new plate in 1973, which would be subject to a longer five-year trial which, if successful again, would finally be replaced by a permanent plate.[16]

★ The iconic yellow-on-black California licence plate of the 1960s, with its AAA-000 format, served as the template for the new British Columbia licence plates introduced in 1970. California had adopted the format after licence plate sizes were standardized in 1955 and their existing 0A00000 format did not fit the new dimensions.[17]

No licence plate book would be complete without an explanation of how the sequence of numbers and letters found on licence plates are determined. In attempting to apply California's AAA-000 format to British Columbia in the late 1960s, the MVB had to contend with the antiquated nature of the equipment at Oakalla. The press had been designed to produce all-numeric licence plates and could therefore only accommodate 10 characters (0 through 9) in each of the six available slots. When the 1970 format required that the first three slots be assigned letters, only 10 could be used. The decision was made to use A, B, C, D, E, F, G, H, J and K, but to exclude the letter I as it too closely resembled the number 1.[18]

The Plate Shop was able to manufacture a block of one million plates using every possible combination with these letters and the numbers 0 through 9. When these plates had been issued and additional stock was required in October of 1971, the Plate Shop switched out the second and third characters with a second block of 10 letters, these being the remainder of the alphabet, including L, M, N, P, R, S, T, V, W, and X (but excluding O, Q, U, Y and Z as they resembled either the numbers 2 and zero, or the letter V). To help differentiate between the 1970 and 1973 series—as the plates would be using the same blue-on-white colour scheme—the first letter in the 1973 series would be from the latter block of letters (between L and X) and would start at LAA-000. This same basic pattern would be repeated in 1979, when the first block of one million plates issued in the new series used only letters A through K (i.e., the first plate issued was AAA-001). In 1985, when the first block of the current flag base was issued, the series started as the 1973 series did, at LAA-001.

★ An example of a plate from the LAA to LKK series issued in 1973.

THE ALL-ZERO FORMAT USED ON SAMPLE PLATES BETWEEN 1924 AND 1969.

AN INVALID 1970 LICENCE PLATE DISPLAYING THREE ZEROS (ISSUED TO COLLECTORS).

★ The Oakalla Plate Shop foreman, Bill Bailey, is shown holding a set of 1973 plates that clearly show the difference between the letters used in 1970 versus 1973 (i.e., the first letter comes from the second half of the alphabet).

BRIAN KENT / *VANCOUVER SUN*

★ BC legislation in the 1960s held that zero did not constitute a valid licence plate number probably to ensure that sample licence plates provided for souvenir purposes could not be construed as lawful plates. Consequently, any plate manufactured with a registration number ending in 000 under the new AAA-000 format was considered to be invalid and could not be issued. Unfortunately, nobody informed the Plate Shop at Oakalla of this restriction and approximately 1,000 sets (or 2,000 individual licence plates) ending in 000 were produced. The MVB eventually disposed of these plates by issuing them as samples to collectors.

A demonstration of the odd way in which this sequencing works is to consider when plates with all three letters the same (i.e., AAA) have been issued. In 2001, when ICBC reversed the position of the numbers and letters and created a new series starting at 000-AAA, it was quite common over the following 18 months to see plates ending with BBB, CCC through to JJJ. The remaining letters, such as LLL, MMM, NNN, PPP and, yes, even XXX, will only be seen within months of the 000-AAA series being exhausted, likely starting in 2013. If ICBC followed a more natural progression when assigning letters, all of these repeating letter combinations would have been spread out more evenly over the past dozen years. The only reason ICBC continues with this pattern is because, administratively, it would be too difficult to issue the plates any other way until a new format is introduced (likely in 2014 after ICBC updates its computer system).

With the experience gained from the 1970 and 1973 series, the MVB was finally ready to issue a permanent plate in 1979. To further reduce the year-end rush at MVB offices, these new licence plates had been designed to accommodate much larger "cyclical decals" that would now include the month of expiry. Although all motorists would receive the same February expiration decal when renewing in 1980, as people continued to buy, sell and scrap vehicles, the expiry month would slowly come to be spread more evenly throughout the year.

Although it had taken the better part of 30 years for a permanent licence plate to come to fruition, the timing proved unfortunate as improvements in printing technology now allowed more elaborate designs to be applied to licence plates at a lower cost. Consequently, a mere five years after the permanent plate's release, the provincial government decided to replace it with a new graphic licence plate. The success of the flag base as a permanent plate is undeniable, but it was never designed to withstand over 25 years of continuous use.

★ The licence plate at left was issued in 1987, and 25 years later is clearly showing its age, but amazingly it was able to be renewed despite the erosion of the characters on the registration number and the complete disappearance of the name of the issuing jurisdiction. The plate at right demonstrates that quality control issues are not always the result of age and can even occur on relatively new plates. Plate No. 882-BDL was issued sometime in 2003 and is showing noticeable deterioration of the reflective sheeting. **E. MORGAN**

The reflective sheeting applied to the plates is only guaranteed for a period of five years, and it is increasingly common to see deteriorating plates, especially those issued in the 1980s. Some jurisdictions, such as Washington, force drivers to surrender their licence plates every seven years to ensure the quality and legibility is maintained for law enforcement purposes. British Columbia has not enacted a similar requirement, but given the unlikelihood of a complete reissuance when the current 000-AAA format is exhausted, ICBC will probably need to adopt a similar policy and require motorists to obtain new plates on a regular basis.

With the shift to permanent plates, the anticipation and excitement surrounding the official announcement of the following year's licence plate colours by the MVB each autumn disappeared. For dedicated plate spotters, however, this thrill still occurs each December with the sighting of a newly registered vehicle sporting the registration decals for the upcoming year. In

★ To help track quality control of the materials used to produce the province's licence plates, a holographic image (also known as a security thread) was added in January of 2011. The serial number in this thread can be used to trace the plant the materials came from—generally the 3M plant in Brownwood, Texas—with the remaining characters revealing the year, month and week.

The holographic image above (BCE1) shows that the materials used in this plate came from Brownwood, Texas, in the first week of February 2010—a full 12 months before it was issued as a licence plate. **E. MORGAN**

★ A regular 1996 registration decal.

★ A replacement 1996 registration decal.

many respects, selecting decal designs and colours has been as fraught for ICBC as the selection of licence plate colours was for the MVB throughout the 1950s and 1960s. Shortly after the introduction of the flag base in 1985, ICBC adopted a standard design along with a rotating series of four colours (green, red, blue and black).

By 1995, computer and home printing technology had progressed to the point where it was relatively easy to reproduce the simple black-on-white colour scheme on the forthcoming year's decal. By the early fall of 1996, the number of counterfeit decals in circulation became so high that ICBC was forced to introduce a new pink-on-white colour scheme for the final two months of the year to stem the flood of fake decals.

Clearing the Air   During the 1991 provincial election campaign, the New Democratic Party (NDP) made a promise to improve Lower Mainland air quality if they were elected. After winning the election, the NDP fulfilled its promise by introducing AirCare, a vehicle emissions testing program designed to keep high smog producers off the road. To ensure compliance, changes were enacted to the legislation so that a vehicle would not be issued new registration decals unless it received a clean bill of health from an AirCare test centre. In typical fashion, most drivers waited until the last possible day before seeking AirCare certification. As there was only a limited number of test stations, daily as opposed to monthly expiration dates became necessary to ease these end-of-the-month rushes. Although AirCare was only mandatory for drivers residing in the Lower Mainland, the use of day decals had the added benefit of further spreading out demand and alleviating rushes at Autoplan agencies throughout the province.[19]

★ Vehicles registered after July of 1993 were required to display a day decal above the flag.

One of the more intriguing questions regarding the future of the licence plate revolves around the continued relevance of registration decals. Over the past decade, British Columbia has been a pioneer in the use of Automatic Licence Plate Recognition (ALPR) technology in Canada—largely thanks to the province becoming a world leader in per capita auto thefts, with Surrey being dubbed the auto theft capital of the world.[20] The technology relies on special software that is able to scan and recognize the characters on licence plates that have been photographed by a camera mounted either within or on the exterior of a police vehicle. Once identified, the information is compared against any number of police databases for stolen vehicles or unlicensed, uninsured or prohibited drivers. An ALPR camera is capable of reading up to 3,000 licence plates per hour, day or night, in all weather and on parked or moving vehicles.[21] The efficiency of the ALPR camera means that decals are quickly becoming inconsequential for identifying whether a vehicle has been properly registered.

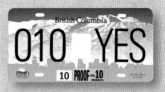

★ In the past, significant community events, such as the 1971 centennial celebrations and Expo 86, have been promoted on registration decals. There was a proposal to include the Olympic logo on the 2010 decals, but this idea was eventually dropped over concerns that the general public should not be forced to advertise the Games on its licence plates. Interestingly, one of the colours considered for the 2010 decal was gold (as in medal), but it was dropped in favour of a "fern green" that was one of the official colours of the Games. The plate shown above is one of the designs considered for use on the Olympic base.

★ When a licence plate is photographed by an ALPR camera, the software that powers the system only analyzes the licence plate characters and discards all other information such as jurisdiction of issue, logos or graphics, and the yearly validation stickers or decals.[22]

Paper Plates

The antithesis of the permanent plate is the Temporary Operating Permit (TOP), which ICBC issued for the first time in 1974 following the decision to have licence plates stay with the owner as opposed to the vehicle.[23] The permits were intended to allow motorists to sell a vehicle from which the licence plates had already been removed, or to buy a new vehicle before selling their current one.

As of 2011, ICBC issues approximately 30,000 such permits a year, which are good anywhere from one to 15 days. The permit consists of two pieces of paper affixed in the front and rear windshields.

By their very nature, the TOPs are easy to counterfeit (the permit shown below is one example). With the increasing prevalence of ALPR technology (which is not well suited to detect the existing type of permit), it is assumed that ICBC will be required to redesign the TOP in the near future.

The most likely alternative would be similar to the temporary permits issued by some US states, such as New Jersey (shown at right, below), which provides its motorists with "poly paper" licence plates that can withstand the elements and last more than 30 days and whose registration numbers are easily visible to law enforcement and ALPR cameras.

★ E. MORGAN (BC) AND JIM MOINI (NEW JERSEY)

After concluding that decals are "obsolete as police are now able to check the validity of a registration plate by computer," Connecticut eliminated its windshield decals in 2010 as part of an effort to save one million dollars a year in administrative, postage and material costs.[24] The state of Western Australia came to the same conclusion when it eliminated the use of decals, while Missouri came close to phasing out decals in 2011 to curb their theft for resale or use on stolen vehicles, which was estimated to cost the state tens of thousands of dollars each year. Before the elimination of registration decals can occur in BC, every police vehicle in the province will need to be equipped with an ALPR camera (at a cost of $20,000 per unit).

ICBC also remains unconvinced about phasing out the use of decals, as British Columbia currently has one of the lowest rates of uninsured motorists in North America.[25] The requirement to display a current decal on a licence plate is considered a significant contributing factor to this statistic, and the costs associated with the decal's continued use might outweigh the costs ICBC could incur if more uninsured vehicles were operating on BC roads. Although the actual amount ICBC spends on decals each year is around $500,000 (a few cents per decal), when administrative costs are factored in, the cost of each decal is closer to two dollars. To reduce this figure, ICBC is constantly exploring other new technologies, including an innovative approach to delivery. Rather than bulk-ordering hundreds of thousands of decals each year and distributing these from ICBC's warehouse to each Autoplan agent, the introduction of a print-on-demand decal system is currently being investigated. A special laser printer, no larger than a telephone and capable of accessing an online database, could be used to print decals when someone renews their insurance with an Autoplan agent. Such a system is currently being tested by 3M in the US and, if successful, could be introduced to British Columbia when a new licence plate series is introduced (possibly in 2014).[26]

We're NOT SO VAIN, ARE WE?

In 2007, the American Association of Motor Vehicle Administrators (AAMVA)—an industry trade group representing the people who oversee the laws governing motor vehicle use—set out to find the vainest drivers in North America. The criteria were simple: officials from each state and province were contacted and asked to identify the percentage of motorists in their jurisdiction who registered a personalized (or "vanity") licence plate. When the results were tabulated and released, it was revealed that only a Texan would be less likely than a British Columbian to affix a personalized licence plate to their vehicle. While British Columbians could now feel a certain satisfaction knowing that they may not be terribly vain—despite the government promoting the province as "The Best Place on Earth"—the survey paints a picture of BC motorists that seems somehow incomplete. For example, in years gone by, British Columbians were some of the most incorrigible licence plate hounds in Canada when it came to seeking out coveted numbers and ultimately lobbying for the introduction of a personalized licence plate program in the late 1970s. Our current aversion to such plates also stands in stark contrast to those in neighbouring jurisdictions, all of whom are far more likely to have registered a personalized slogan. Yet if we consider recent trends in licence plate marketing elsewhere, our future could likely be a much vainer one, and we need only look at our past to appreciate why.

After Massachusetts introduced an annual licence plate in 1903, low numbers that had been assigned years earlier once again became available as the registration list was always restarted at the beginning of the year. For motorists who believed that a low number conveyed status or exclusivity, or that a certain combination of numbers would bring luck, the competition to acquire these numbers became intense, especially as the number of motorists grew exponentially during the first decades of the 20th century. Quick to recognize the value of these numbers, politicians in New York and Vermont set about withdrawing all low numbers from general circulation so that they could be distributed as political favours. Number 1, the most coveted of numbers, however, was usually reserved for the exclusive use of a state's governor. In order to legitimize this system and deal with the flood of requests from motorists seeking not only low and lucky numbers but also birthdays, addresses and phone numbers, many jurisdictions instituted "reserve lists" that limited the range of numbers that could be requested. Massachusetts is known to have implemented such a list in 1911, and British Columbia would follow suit a few years later, but with one notable difference: no plates were ever held back for political purposes.[1] Granted, most of the province's early motorists were business and political elites, so there was no need to withhold low numbers as these were already in their possession. Nevertheless, the MVB was able to implement a policy of assigning numbers on a first-come, first-served basis with no right of transfer, creating a level playing field.

Eventually, the MVB allowed motorists who had registered a specific number the year before to have that same number the following year, as long as their registration hadn't lapsed. If it had lapsed, that number would be reassigned to the first person to ask for it. Inevitably, motorists wanting to hold on to their beloved numbers or hoping to stake a claim on any

new available numbers would form a long line outside the MVB's Victoria head office the night before the new plates went on sale.

Year after year, requests for plate No. 1 were the most common, but in the six decades that this number was issued, it changed owners less than a handful of times before finally being acquired—under questionable circumstances—by the provincial Public Works Department. The first vehicle to display the No. 1 was the Orient Buckboard belonging to John Barnsley. Barnsley would retain the No. 1 until his death in 1924, at which point the question of rights to it became somewhat murky.

Four years later, the MVB received 88 requests seeking No. 1, including one from the widow of a doctor who had been the holder of the plate the previous year. While the MVB's decision on Mrs. Miller's request remains a mystery, by the 1930s General Noel Money, renowned builder and proprietor of the Qualicum Beach Hotel on Vancouver Island, had acquired the No. 1 plate. Money would display the number until 1938, when the Department of Public Works managed to submit its application first and was assigned the plate before Money could lodge his own application. Oddly, Money was widely known to apply to the MVB weeks early to ensure he did not lose the No. 1, and under the MVB's own "special request" policy he should have retained the rights to it. For its part, the Province wanted to attach the number to the official government vehicle used for transporting the premier, visiting dignitaries and other notables such as the senior naval officer of the Pacific Fleet. Money had to settle for a different number in 1938 and passed away the following year.[2]

★ When President Franklin Delano Roosevelt visited Victoria on September 30, 1937, he was chauffeured through the city with Lieutenant-Governor Eric Hamber in the official government vehicle that sported the rather pedestrian licence plate No. 3486.

The following year the Province would obtain, under somewhat questionable circumstances, the coveted No. 1 licence plate for use on this vehicle. **IMAGE A-00828 COURTESY OF ROYAL BC MUSEUM, BC ARCHIVES**

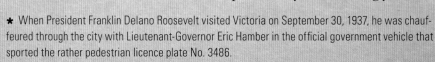

The Province would continue to actively use No. 1 on vehicles through the early 1950s but changed this practice following the demise of the Thunderbird plates in 1954.

It was not just low numbers that were sought. By 1923, the MVB was fielding requests for numbers as high as 8,000. Within a few years the competition for numbers became so intense that the MVB limited available numbers to those between 1 and 7,000. Yet even this proved unwieldy, and the list was subsequently reduced to 3,000 to decrease the administrative burden. Some of the unusual and varied numbers that appealed to motorists were combinations inspired by poker hands (1111 represented four aces), bridge hands, historic dates (with the conquest dates of 1066 and 1492 being particularly in vogue with history teachers), phone numbers, birthdays and house addresses.[3]

Having connections did not guarantee a specific number, but it did not hurt. The mayor of Vancouver, William Malkin, requested as low a licence plate number as was available in 1930 for use on his Packard Coupe. Whereas other motorists who had submitted similar requests at the same time as the mayor were assigned numbers above 3,000, Malkin was assigned No. 53. Minister of Finance William Shelly requested and received licence plate 4444 for his Franklin Coupe that same year. Even Duff Pattullo, premier from 1933 to 1941, displayed plate 951 on his personal vehicle during his time in office. This happened to be the same number as his residential address on Beach Drive in Victoria.[4]

Wesley Black, Provincial Secretary in the early 1960s, reportedly sought out plate 54 at the behest of his children, who were avid viewers of the television show *Car 54, Where Are You?* As the story goes, the best the MVB could

★ This run of No. 1 plates was retained by the MVB between 1956 and 1969 and hung on the wall of the Victoria office as a memento. The plates were discovered at the adjacent provincial legislative buildings in the 1990s. GREG IVERSON

★ It is rumoured that a sales representative of the Heinz Company routinely reserved plate No. 57 (for obvious reasons), while a representative of the Parker Pen Company sought out No. 51, in honour of the company's bestselling pen, but he was too late.[5]

★ When the first automobile arrived in Prince Rupert in 1909, the fellow behind the wheel was Thomas Dufferin Pattullo, future premier of the province. First elected to the legislature in 1916, by 1932 Pattullo was leader of the Opposition and had just moved house to 951 Beach Drive in Victoria. Pattullo's new home was situated on the doorstep of the Victoria golf course. "After his early morning round he left the house for work . . . He took great pleasure in tooling along Beach Drive in his brand new Nash sedan to his office in the legislative building, and his good nature lasted all day. Both the drive and the destination were among the joys of his life."[6]

IMAGE PDP00451 COURTESY OF ROYAL BC MUSEUM, BC ARCHIVES, PRINCE RUPERT CITY & REGIONAL ARCHIVES, J. D. ALLEN PHOTOGRAPHIC COMPANY FONDS, P990-26-5271

First Motor Car in Prince Rupert. May 1909.

★ In the 1940s, Premier John Hart was issued plate No. 15000 for use on his private vehicle.[7] IMAGE B-08419 COURTESY OF ROYAL BC MUSEUM, BC ARCHIVES

★ Lawrie Wallace, the chair of the province's Centennial Committee, displayed plate No. 100 from 1957 through to 1969 in recognition of the work he had done in organizing celebrations to honour the founding of the Crown Colony of British Columbia in 1858. WALLACE FAMILY

produce was No. 52, which happened to be the first year Black had been elected to the legislature and the year that his party came to power—so he accepted.[8]

When letters first began to appear on passenger licence plates across North America in the 1920s, the opportunities for personalization increased. Connecticut was likely the first jurisdiction to issue a personalized licence plate (one in which letters are arranged to spell a word or name). In 1937, the state began to allow motorists who had maintained a good driving record for five years to display plates with their initials or a name comprised of up to three letters. By the 1950s, states such as Ohio and New York had introduced similar programs by stipulating that a set of special conditions be met before a motorist could qualify to select a three-letter registration. New Hampshire threw the doors open in 1957 when it allowed motorists to apply for a slogan of their own choosing for a small fee. The following year, Vermont allowed its motorists to choose combinations containing both letters and numbers. In 1970, California introduced personalized licence plates with a twist—10 dollars from the 25-dollar fee was earmarked for a special fund to fight pollution. The first California vanity plate issued by Governor Ronald Reagan was AMIGO because it sounded friendly, and by 1977 over $18 million had been raised. These innovations paved the way for the explosive growth of vanity licence plate programs throughout the United States and Canada, starting in the 1970s.[9]

George Gregory, the Liberal MLA for Victoria, put forward a suggestion in the late 1950s that would have introduced personalized licence plates to British Columbia in an attempt to exploit the growing demand for numbers from the MVB's reserve list. For 5 dollars, motorists could have a simple plate with a special number; for 10 dollars, they could have initials, "such as that of their girlfriend," put on a plate. Gregory predicted that, if this program were implemented, "there would be line-ups of motorists with $5 and $10 bills in their hands." Given the thousands of motorists seeking numbers from the reserve list, if an application fee had been successfully introduced in British Columbia, the financial windfall for the province would have been substantial. Yet no such program was ever implemented. That Gregory was an Opposition member of the legislature in the era of W.A.C. Bennett's Social Credit may partially explain why the government did not take up the suggestion, but there are other clues. The premature demise of the Thunderbird plate only three years earlier was certainly a contributing factor as the unfamiliar array of letters and numbers used in the serial had soured the MVB on alpha-numeric plates. Not only had the letters complicated the MVB's filing systems, but law enforcement officials found it difficult to identify vehicles sporting the plates. Press reports of the day also revealed that the Province was strongly considering abolishing letters on passenger plates altogether.[10] Rather tellingly, only when vehicle registrations neared the one million mark in 1970 did the MVB consent to the reappearance of letters.[11]

By 1966, the number of people seeking numbers from the reserve list had skyrocketed from a somewhat manageable 1,800 in 1946 to an astonishing 35,000.[12] The administrative cost to the MVB of sorting through tens of thousands of applications for fewer than 3,000 plates was completely unsustainable, but an apparent solution to the problem was about to present itself. The all-numeric six-digit serial format (i.e., 000-000) that the province had used since the demise of the Thunderbird base in 1955 was nearing exhaustion as the number of motor vehicles registered in British Columbia slowly progressed towards the one million mark. In preparing for the transition to a new AAA-000 combination in 1970, Attorney General Leslie Peterson was adamant that the end of the all-numeric format would also mark the end of the special reserve list, as it was proving to be "a big expense to the taxpayer to service a small number of people."[13]

The 1970 licence plate series had been intended as a test to see if a permanent plate validated through the use of plastic registration decals could succeed. If the plates proved successful during an initial two- to three-year trial period—which they did—then a five-year or possibly permanent plate would be introduced. When a new licence plate series was released in 1973, its colour and layout were virtually indistinguishable from those of its predecessor, save one important exception. Instead of recommencing the series at AAA-001, the MVB opted to simply pick up from where the 1970 series had finished, which was after the letter K. Accordingly, the first plate issued in 1973 was LAA-001, which clearly did not carry the same cachet as a plate beginning with AAA. More significantly, the MVB's head office in Victoria did not receive the first block of plates in the series, breaking a 60-year tradition that stretched back to the first annual plates issued in 1913. Some wondered whether this was done to avoid the bad publicity the MVB had received three years earlier following the "disappearance" of plate AAA-001. But according to Keith Jackman, who was managing the MVB's Abbotsford office at the time, there was nothing untoward about this change in distribution. Director of Vehicle Registration and Licensing Denny Heinike sent the first 16,000 sets in the series to Jackman's office as Abbotsford was first on his alphabetical list.[14] In place of their traditional low numbers, Victoria residents now had plates starting in the VAA-001 to VKK-999 range, a decision that Ray Hadfield, the Superintendent of Motor Vehicles at the time, further attributed to the need for a clean block of 100,000 plates for the Capital region. Some indignant motorists complained about their issued letter combinations—VD, for example, could be construed as short for "Venereal Disease" (to which one wag noted, Victoria was a port city). Others, however, tried to put a positive spin on matters by interpreting VD as "Victoria District."[15] Either way, the era of the low-numbered plate in British Columbia had effectively ended as the advent of the permanent plate meant that there would no longer be a "next year" for those hoping to obtain a coveted number for their vehicle.

★ "Receiving plates from clerk John Bailey is Mrs. Gwynne Thompson." For the first time ever, Victorians were not issued the first block of licence plates in 1973—that honour went to Abbotsford, based on its alphabetic advantage. In place of the first block of plates, Victoria motorists received sets starting with V.

ALEX BARTA / VICTORIA TIMES COLONIST

Where in the World is AAA-001?

When the reserve list was abolished in 1970, it did little to discourage Victoria resident Bruce Roger, who had been following newspaper stories about the new plates throughout the fall and early winter of 1969. Roger specifically recalled reading that no MVB employee would be permitted to put aside any plate in advance of the public release on Monday, January 4, 1970, and, consequently, felt that if he could be the first person in line that day he had a good chance of receiving the first plate—AAA-001. Thinking it would be "kind of crazy but fun to see if we could get the first plate," Roger and his cousin (who was hoping to obtain plate AAA-007), set out for the MVB office on Menzies Street. Showing up at about 11:30 the night before, the two were the first to arrive and started the queue "armed with warm jackets, chairs, a few snacks, and nothing else." The next person did not arrive for another 30 minutes, and after chatting for a while, Roger and his cousin struck a bargain with the fellow, agreeing that he could have any number he wished except 001 and 007. This arrangement was repeated over the next several hours as more people started to join the line. As morning came and MVB employees began to file into the office, a clerk purportedly flashed the coveted first plate to the group waiting outside. Yet when the doors finally opened at 8:30 a.m. and Roger walked up to the wicket and handed over his papers and money, the plate he was presented with was AAA-003!

"When I recovered from my shock, it was explained to me that the first two plates were already sold," Roger recalls. "I tried to reason with the person there, explaining that we'd been there all night, 001 was guaranteed to the first person there, which was undoubtedly me, and I wasn't leaving until I got it. But all my protesting and even the support of all the people in the line with us was to no avail. They simply said the first two plates were gone and that was that." Grudgingly, Roger took AAA-003 along with the other plates for his relatives (his cousin was able to obtain 007) and returned home.

★ Bruce Roger beside the AAA-003 licence plate that he was issued after waiting in line all night outside the Motor Vehicle Branch's main office on Menzies Street in Victoria. *VICTORIA TIMES COLONIST* ★ Above is a representation of the AAA-001 plate that was issued to an employee of the Liquor Control Board.

Word of the incident travelled fast, and later that day a reporter from a local newspaper tracked Roger down at work and began asking some questions. Soon, reports on the radio and in the newspapers featured rampant speculation about what had happened to AAA-001 and AAA-002. For two weeks, the MVB remained silent on the subject, conceding only that the plates had been legally issued, but not to any MVB employees. Adding to the mystery was a rumour that the people with the plates were afraid to take their cars out of their garages for fear of being identified, and it would be several months before they were seen on local roads. Finally, it was revealed that a clerk with the Liquor Control Board (LCB) had been awarded plate AAA-001, while AAA-002 had gone to a member of the Canadian Armed Forces. The LCB routinely loaned employees to the MVB to assist with the January rush, an opportunity this LCB employee used to his or her advantage. Almost 40 years later, Roger recalls being told that the person or persons responsible had been reprimanded, but this did not make up for the fact that his adventure had been ruined.[16]

Not to be deterred, and seeking an outlet for their creative impulses, motorists from across the province started a grassroots letter-writing campaign, lobbying the provincial government to introduce personalized licence plates. After receiving hundreds of these requests himself, Premier Bill Bennett finally announced in May of 1978 that he supported licence plates that carried unique messages, names or numbers and would shortly be presenting a proposal to his cabinet.[17]

Settling on the design of the plate turned out to be only one of the MVB's many challenges as it attempted to set up the personalized plate program. In the weeks leading up to July 1, 1979, the MVB was optimistic that approximately 20,000 applications would be submitted within the first year of the program, half in the first three months.[18] This was not unrealistic given the tens of thousands of motorists who, throughout the 1960s, had been applying on an annual basis for numbers from the relatively small reserve list of 3,000 plate numbers. With multiple combinations of letters and numbers now available, the sky would be the limit in terms of applicants (and revenue). By the

Vanity Graphics

One of the curious aspects of BC's personalized licence plate—at least for those who think about these sorts of things—has always been why the province opted to introduce a unique design, and how it came to settle upon the now familiar "mountains and sea" backdrop. Every other state or province that issued vanity plates simply used their regular passenger base plate design. As BC had just introduced new passenger plates in January of 1979, it would have been logical to use the same design for personalized plates. Yet, when it was unveiled in late 1979, the personalized plate displayed what was considered to be a cutting-edge graphic design showcasing the province's rugged geography.

★ In 1979, British Columbia introduced a new licence plate design (at left) for passenger vehicles, but opted to use a distinct design for the personalized licence plate (at right) introduced later that same year.

The cabinet felt that motorists should get something special in return for the extra fees they were going to have to pay to obtain the plates—hence the decision to create a unique design, a task that initially fell to MVB staff. It was not long, however, before a number of cabinet ministers began to get in on the action by submitting their own designs. Keith Jackman recalls one design proposed by Grace McCarthy, a prominent member of the government who had been a florist prior to entering politics. The wild collage of flowers layout she favoured did not allow for the proper placement of personalized slogans and was ultimately rejected. Having already seen a number of proposals rejected by the cabinet, Jackman and Gig Sinclair, a representative of 3M, were returning to Victoria on the ferry from Vancouver, contemplating the forests, sea and mountains theme that the government wanted to incorporate on the plate. Realizing that the scenery of the coast they were passing by might meet all of the cabinet's criteria for the plate, the two produced a rough sketch. Sinclair took this sketch to a professional design artist at 3M who made it presentable to the minister. When Alex Fraser saw the mock-up of the plate, he agreed to include it along with four others being considered by the cabinet. The politicians had now found their plate, and when asked if he thought at the time that this design would last for better than 30 years and become an almost iconic British Columbia image, Jackman just shakes his head.[19]

middle of August, however, only 1,400 people had applied for the plates. Alex Fraser was surprised considering the pressure his ministry had been under in the years leading up to the introduction of the program. He chalked the sluggish uptake of the plates to a lack of publicity and was hopeful that a surge in demand would occur once the first plates were distributed in September 1979.[20] Yet, as the month of September came and went, it was announced that a "design snarl" had delayed the plates but that the minister was hopeful (yet again) to have a sample to unveil in November.[21]

Behind the scenes, the introduction of the licence plates had run into a number of problems. As Jackman recalls, a contributing factor was a freeze that the Treasury Board had put on the ministries purchasing new computers. To begin processing the applications for personalized plates, the MVB would need new equipment, and it fell to Jackman to make a case for buying a word processor and shepherding this through the provincial bureaucracy. At the same time, the MVB was developing a list of "taboo words" that could be input into the new computer and would be ready before any applications were processed. In fact, the MVB was so determined to ensure that no double entendres slipped through that officials were using mirrors and computers to catch any off-colour requests. Motor vehicle agencies in Texas, California and Oregon had forwarded their lists of prohibited words to the MVB—a process that resulted in an initial compilation of 1,500 words. To this, MVB employees added another 1,500 words. According to the program coordinator, they "had to be in a really dirty frame of mind to do this job properly." Finally, each request was run through a computer at the University of Victoria that was capable of identifying offensive words in foreign languages. So successful were the MVB's efforts in compiling its list that it would be adopted by all of the other Canadian provinces as well as a few American states. Offending words in 1979 included DOPE, MAFIA, CANADA, JESUS and NDP, while all

★ In September of 1973, the California Department of Motor Vehicles (DMV) introduced a new policy that allowed it to recall an "offensive" slogan. One of the first to be targeted was Encino resident Burt Blum's slogan, UP URZ2 (Up Yours Too). The list of offensive slogans that the DMV subsequently compiled would be shared with the MVB ahead of the introduction of a similar personalized plate program in British Columbia.

JOHN MALMIN, COPYRIGHT © 1973. *LOS ANGELES TIMES*. REPRINTED WITH PERMISSION

★ Richard Rogers of White Rock proudly displaying the first vanity licence plate—HEALEY —issued in British Columbia.

IAN MCKAIN / *VICTORIA TIMES COLONIST*

references to sex, drugs, liquor and racial or political groups were forbidden. Moreover, under the legislation enabling the issuance of personalized plates, the superintendent could recall any licence plate deemed "unseemly, vulgar, indecent or offensive" (but more on this later).[22] When the official unveiling ceremony for the plate was held on December 6, 1979, the minister presented the first personalized plate, HEALEY, to Richard Rogers of White Rock for use on his Austin-Healey sports car.[23]

The policing of vanity slogans is a tricky business and something that bedevils issuing authorities throughout North America. The legislation that governs ICBC provides the corporation with the quasi-judicial authority to refuse a particular slogan if it is unseemly, vulgar, indecent, offensive or distracting to other drivers. Less well known is the fact that ICBC also retains the right to revoke a plate that has already been issued if, in the future, the slogan gains an objectionable or misleading connotation. It is not clear how many times ICBC has felt compelled to pull a plate off the road, but there are a couple of known instances where questionable slogans had to be dealt with.

Early in the life of the program, the slogan FUBAR was issued. As World War II veterans and fans of the movie *Saving Private Ryan* know, this stands for "**F**ucked **U**p **B**eyond **A**ll **R**ecognition." Needless to say, the plate was quickly recalled.[24] More recently, ICBC found itself caught out by three seemingly innocuous letters: WTF. In the parlance of text messages, the letters are an acronym for "What The Fuck." Although WTF is listed in the Internet Acronyms Dictionary (a web search tool popular with slogan censors), it somehow slipped past ICBC, and a car bearing the off-colour acronym was spotted in mid-2008.

Offending slogans are usually caught before ever being stamped onto a licence plate. During the first year of the program, of the 2,000 applications that were submitted, a total of 55 were rejected, including IMEASY, IM4SEX and GORF ("frog" spelled backwards—a cultural insult).[25] For what seemed to be obvious reasons, the MVB also rejected a request for the word HOOKER. However, the applicant, whose surname was Hooker, threatened to sue the MVB over the rejection and the slogan was ultimately issued. For a few years afterwards, the MVB decided that applicants could have a dubious slogan on their plate only if it was the exact spelling of their name, but this has been discarded since ICBC took over administration of the program. For example, an application for KILL was submitted on the basis that this was the applicant's last name, but ICBC deemed it inappropriate and rejected the request.[26]

One of the more peculiar slogan flaps occurred in the mid-1990s when ICBC began to receive complaints about the slogan WE LOG. Only a few years earlier, provincial forestry practices at Clayoquot Sound on Vancouver Island had led to mass demonstrations, arrests and national news headlines. Public sentiment on the issue of logging was undoubtedly still raw when the slogan, which was no longer even affixed to a vehicle, appeared in the printed instructions for registration decals that Autoplan dealers distributed to motorists (see right).

According to ICBC, "the logger-logo seemed like a good idea at the time . . . [as] the original plate had been returned by a logging company . . . so it happened to be lying in the office."[27] Changing public attitudes, however, forced ICBC to change the slogan in the illustration to SAMPLE—which has yet to offend anyone.

★ What the @$#% is this?

E. MORGAN

★ *VANCOUVER PROVINCE*

Over the years, the number of slogans rejected by ICBC has steadily increased as the corporation's censorship activities have extended beyond religion, politics, ethnic slurs, sex, narcotics and good-natured bathroom humour (what's wrong with stating IHAV2P?) and into the realm of street racing terminology. Why this is raises very interesting questions. Our neighbours south of the border, with their First Amendment right to freedom of speech and their

litigious propensities, have thoroughly explored the issue of state censorship of vanity slogans.[28] One theory holds that slogans deemed objectionable by ICBC reflect cultural fears as well as regional psychoses, which are "often arbitrary and reflective of the personal tastes of one or more powerful individuals within a bureaucracy who try to act as guardians of public decency."[29] One could argue that ICBC's sensitivity to street racing terminology and slogans is an overreaction to the rash of accidents and deaths from street racing that plagued Lower Mainland streets at the turn of the century. The more likely reason stems from a potential conflict in ICBC's mandate of registering *and* insuring vehicles. About $100 million per year is spent on road safety projects throughout the province, and allowing street racing slogans on licence

★ The changing mores of vanity plate etiquette at ICBC is best exemplified by the issuance of the WEXLR8 slogan in 1980— to an employee of the Motor Vehicle Branch, no less! Between 2004 and 2007, ICBC would deny seven requests for iterations of this same slogan (XLR8TN, XLR8N, XLR8, IEXLR8 and IXLR8) on the basis that they were "speed/racing related" and therefore objectionable.
ROSS MASEN / *VANCOUVER PROVINCE*

★ Establishing the line between acceptable and offensive political messages can be challenging. Case in point, the overtly political NO GST issued to Bill Phelps in 1990 (above). **WAYNE LEIDENFROST / *VANCOUVER PROVINCE*** ★ At right, a disgruntled resident of West Vancouver added his or her own political message to the personalized licence plates of Mayor D. Humphreys in 1986.
COLIN PRICE / *VANCOUVER PROVINCE*

plates is seen to be an inconsistent initiative.[30] The effectiveness of censoring licence plate slogans in an attempt to reduce the occurrence of street racing (and insurance claims) is unclear. From a policy perspective, denying requests for 2 FAST, GUNNIT and IXLR8T is probably negligible in addressing the broader issue of street racing.

The cost of censorship is not always inconsequential. In 2008, South Dakota contemplated abandoning its vanity licence plate program altogether, as the costs of having to defend a single court challenge of a refused slogan had the potential to eat up all of the revenue generated by the sale of such plates in that state.[31] While it is unlikely that a single challenge of a refused slogan would present a budgetary crisis for ICBC, measures have been implemented to avoid costly litigation, such as the introduction in 2001 of an ombudsman (known as the fairness commissioner), who is tasked with reviewing contested decisions, including rejected slogans. Yet in the first 10 years that this position has existed, the commissioner has never been asked to review a rejected slogan, despite ICBC dispatching over 200 slogans a year on the grounds of their perceived inappropriateness.

So why is it that British Columbians have never warmed to the personalized licence plate? While the introduction of a 75-dollar fee likely dampened many motorists' enthusiasm, this does not really explain the now decades-long disdain of BC drivers towards the concept of vanity plates. In other parts of the world, motorists are quite willing to part with absurd amounts of money for "cherished numbers," "heritage plates" or any other coveted combination of letters and numbers.

What sets BC apart—or back, depending upon one's point of view—has been ICBC's inability to create or respond to market demand, which is largely related to its funding arrangement with the provincial government. All revenues collected from sales and renewals of personalized plates are handed over to the provincial government, while the costs of administering the program

★ A rarity in terms of personalized plates, these seven-digit slogans were once issued to employees of ICBC on the occasion of their retirement.

★ A familiar sight for frequent passengers of BC Ferries, these full-length colour advertisements for the Olympic licence plates could be found on the elevator doors located on the car decks. Due to current funding arrangements with the provincial government, there is no incentive for ICBC to undertake similar promotional initiatives for the personalized licence plate, such as billboards on Highway 1 (another favourite spot for Olympic plate advertising).

are covered by ICBC and ultimately borne by all motorists through their insurance rates. This arrangement creates a perverse disincentive for ICBC, ensuring the program is not successful. Outdated computer systems make administration of the plates time-consuming and therefore expensive, and any marketing, promotion or change to the design of the plate would require an increase in insurance rates to cover these costs.[32] The irony of this situation is, of course, that the personalized plate program was originally devised to be a revenue generator.

Looking forward, ICBC is in the midst of updating its computer systems through its Transformation 2014 initiative, which should make administration more efficient. Ideally, the funding arrangement with the provincial government will improve—possibly becoming similar to that used with the Olympic specialty plate—contributing to lower insurance rates for motorists and encouraging innovations with sales potential. Such innovations would play to the strengths of the plates, which is the "vanity" of the motorists who want them. The introduction of a seventh or even an eighth digit has proven to increase the sale of vanity plates in other jurisdictions.[33] If slogans aren't catching the imagination of motorists, ICBC could look at resurrecting the coveted No. 1 or the reserve list abandoned after 1969. Some of the most ridiculous amounts of money spent on vanity plates in other countries involve low numbers.

It is not surprising that the AAMVA survey found Virginians to be the vainest motorists in all of North America, as a choice in background designs increases the likelihood of motorists opting for personalization—and in Virginia motorists can choose from over 400 different backgrounds. Yet, in British Columbia, when the Province introduced the Veteran (2004) and Olympic (2007) specialty plates, motorists were not allowed the option of personalizing them. Even something as simple as allowing people to choose the standard passenger design has not been pursued.

Should there be another vanity licence plate survey, British Columbia will likely find itself at the very back of the pack. In a first for North America, Texas took the bold step of privatizing the design and marketing of its vanity plates in 2008.[34] A private company, MyPlates, now handles all such plate orders and, for the first time, is offering motorists in the Lone Star State a choice of dozens of different background themes and colours, seven-digit slogans, the use of corporate names, variable pricing, online ordering and the ability to print out a paper copy of a plate to see how it will look on a vehicle. A number of potentially desirable seven-letter words have been set aside by the company for potential auction to the highest bidder (imagine what CANUCKS could fetch at auction). In British Columbia, however, the status quo prevails.

The COST of PROVINCE BUILDING

6

Building roads in British Columbia has never been an easy or inexpensive task and has plagued governments since the founding of the Crown Colony in the 1850s. As one observer has noted, "The importance of a good road system to the province has always been recognised, but the will to create it has been fickle."[1] As automobiles became more numerous, the roads they drove on were nothing more than the wagon trails that had been constructed decades earlier. To advance the cause of "Good Roads" everywhere, motorists began to form advocacy groups such as the Vancouver Automobile Club and Pacific Highway Association. The lobbying of these groups eventually led to roads being paved between Vancouver and New Westminster, Chilliwack and Hope and New Westminster and Blaine, Washington.[2] One of the provincial government's main challenges in attempting to answer the call for better roads was the comparatively paltry revenues generated from licensing fees. When economic conditions worsened throughout the 1930s and 1940s, road building virtually ceased throughout the province.[3] It would start up again in the 1950s following the election of the Social Credit Party under W.A.C. Bennett, who increased spending on highway and bridge construction exponentially. Capital expenditures on these items would rise from approximately $16 million in 1951 to $35 million by 1955, and finally to over $80 million a year—or more than 20 percent of the total provincial budget—by the late 1950s.[4] As the premier was inclined to boast,

> The greatest highway-building program, not just in British Columbia's history but per capita in the entire western world, has been accomplished without borrowing at all . . . in fact, the Social Credit government has moved more rock and other materials and spent more on highways in the past six years—and paid for every cent of it—than all previous British Columbia governments did in the first ninety-four years of our history.[5]

Dubbed a "blacktop government," Social Credit's focus on road building was a necessary first step to the eventual opening of the province to large-scale resource development. By 1958, 825 miles of new highway had been constructed, with a further 5,700 miles either rebuilt, improved, surfaced or resurfaced.[6] According to Bennett's Minister of Highways, "Flyin' Phil" Gaglardi, "every year in the wintertime in the interior, people used to jack their cars up off their wheels and block them up and leave them there for the winter, because they didn't maintain the highway in the winter time. I said to the licensing department, 'Do you sell a licence for half a year? You sell them for the whole year; therefore from now on the highways remain open all year'— and I saw to it that they did."[7]

As the Socreds' aggressive road-building program began to wind down at the end of the decade, the government had to contend with the costs of maintaining this new road system. For the 1959 registration year, there were approximately 420,000 vehicles for a provincial population of 1,580,000, and the fees collected from road-user charges only covered about 54 percent of net road costs.[8] This meant that people who didn't use the roads, or the average taxpayers, were shouldering a disproportionate amount of the costs. Even more troubling was that of the 54 percent being collected from road users, private

Good Roads Everywhere Towards the end of the 19th century, a plethora of organizations dedicated to the improvement of the motoring experience in the United States sprang up and began advocating for an improved road system. Given the woeful state of the province's roads at this time, a Good Roads League was formed in British Columbia to similarly advocate for an improved road system.

A prominent player in the American movement was Charles Henry Davis, who established the National Highways Association in 1911. As a promotional idea, Davis convinced all of the (then) 48 American states; the territories of Alaska and Hawaii; six "dependencies" (such as Guam and Puerto Rico); all of the (then) nine Canadian provinces; the Yukon Territory; Newfoundland; and other hemispheric countries (such as Panama), to provide him with a licence plate from their jurisdiction featuring the No. 25, which he attached to a Hudson that he drove across the continent.

Rumour has it that when Davis died in 1951, his collection of No. 25 licence plates covered the walls of a carriage house found on his property. Later, the state government would acquire the property for the purpose of constructing a new road across Cape Cod. At this point, it is believed that the plates began to disperse into the hands of various collectors.

By an order-in-council, Davis received a pair of No. 25 BC plates each year throughout the 1920s and 1930s. Rather than revoke the BC No. 25 plate sent to Mr. Davis, the MVB simply produced an additional set for use by a motorist in BC. Consequently, it is not unusual to find more than two No. 25 plates for any given year between 1922 and 1940. It is also somewhat difficult to distinguish between plates used by Mr. Davis and those of the lawfully registered BC motorist.

★ A 1924 British Columbia No. 25 licence plate is visible among the plates attached to the side of the vehicle (beside a 1924 New Brunswick and above the 1924 Oregon E-25). *MOTOR TRAVEL MAGAZINE*

passenger vehicles were contributing over 60 percent, with the remainder being collected from commercial vehicle operators. Yet commercial vehicles were seen to place a greater strain on the road system because they were larger and heavier than passenger vehicles. By not having to pay an equitable share of the costs associated with maintaining the road network, commercial vehicle operators were also seen to be unfairly benefiting over other modes of transportation, such as railways. For the government, this raised an important policy question about the degree to which road costs should be covered by the user versus the non-user; and of those users, how much should be paid by commercial vehicles.[9] To help answer these questions, a Royal Commission of Inquiry, comprising four senior members of the public service, was established in 1958.

The commission found that the scale of licence fees levied on commercial vehicle operators had last been reviewed in 1934, while the tax on gasoline had remained at 10 cents a gallon since 1947. Not surprisingly, these fees no longer generated enough revenue to cover the costs of the new road system that had been constructed by the Socreds. More troubling was the realization that the highway system lacked basic safeguards to ensure commercial vehicle weights did not exceed authorized limits, that loopholes in the classification of vehicles were routinely exploited, and that licence fees were being evaded or avoided on a regular basis. The commission would make a number of recommendations, but the most significant was that overall road-user charges should be somewhere in the range of 66 percent and that commercial vehicles should bear at least half of these costs. If these recommendations were implemented, commercial operators faced a fee increase of 33 percent.

One of the specific loopholes that the commission tackled was related to industrial vehicle licence plates, which had been introduced in 1957. The intent of these new X-prefix plates was to allow vehicles engaged in road construction and maintenance or industrial undertakings (such as in the mining industry) to use the road system at a reduced rate, as these vehicles were not considered to be regular road users.

★ In the picture above, a drilling machine is doing road work on Quadra Street in Victoria (1960).

★ Following amendments to the Motor Carrier Act in 1959, the XH prefix was discontinued, as dump trucks were excluded from the list of qualified vehicles.

The following year, amendments to the Motor Carrier Act inadvertently created a loophole that was quickly exploited by dump-truck operators, who could now register their vehicles with either an X or XH plate and drive significant distances to a work site, where they would compete and occasionally undercut local truck operators who did not qualify for this exemption and had to register under the act and pay the additional licensing fees. The commissioners were also concerned that these operators were evading tax by registering with X plates, and that the list of eligible vehicles needed to be restricted. To deal with this, the commissioners recommended that the government "exclude dump-trucks . . . from the list of vehicles for which these plates may be obtained and to require them to pay full fees if they use the roads at all."[10] The Province acted on this recommendation; dump trucks were excluded from qualifying for these plates, and the XH prefix was phased out. Over half a century later, X plates can easily be spotted at any road construction project throughout the province.

The Socreds' road-building program had occurred against a backdrop of transformation within the forest industry, as steam was quickly being replaced by technological advances in trucks and power saws that allowed loggers to access steeper grades and open new areas—especially in coastal forests.[11] By the mid-1950s, many logging camps had switched from the use of railway lines to trucks, and with this the logger's way of life and role in local communities began to change:

> With a road to the outside world, he was free to live away from his job . . . From a single "Tame Ape" whose only approach to a home was a camp bunkhouse, he became a family man with wife and child, house and mortgage. He ceased to be a bird-of-passage between the monastic confines of the woods and the fleshpots of Vancouver. Unionized and well-paid, his working conditions vastly improved, he became a pillar of his community.[12]

Despite the fact that forestry was the largest industry in the province in the 1950s and increasingly reliant on commercial vehicle transportation, logging truck operators had not taken the Royal Commission seriously and had largely been absent during the hearings held throughout 1959. This was attributed to a common practice that had developed among many small operators to disregard existing regulations and, by extension, government inquiries. Part of the problem was that commercial vehicle fees had remained unchanged for decades. This existing two-dollar fee was considered nominal, as it did not even cover the administrative costs of issuing a permit and was an insufficient deterrent to protect the highway system from excessive loads. Moreover, the issuance of overweight permits had become so commonplace that they were described by some as a "licence to disobey the law." When the commission's recommendation of additional weigh stations and more rigid enforcement of existing rules was acted upon for the 1960 licensing year, it was quickly revealed that breaches by logging truck operators of regulations limiting size and weight were epidemic.[13]

Even though the ranching and freight delivery industries were by no means happy with the Royal Commission's recommendations, it was the storm of criticism from logging truck operators that prompted Transport Minister Lyle Wicks to reconvene the Royal Commission in February of 1960.[14] Fellow politicians Hugh Shirreff (Skeena) and Cyril Shelford (Omineca) had already been telling their colleagues that "everybody in their constituencies was suffering . . . that the tax setup was an injustice." Shelford added that his "whole area is based on logging and logging trucks. If it were not for that we'd be dead in a week . . . [and the] new regulations [have] raised payments in some cases from $53 to around $140 for [licences]."[15] Unlike 1958, when the commissioners went on the road in the summer of 1960 their hearings would be dominated

★ Visible on this logging truck are both 1936 Commercial licence plate No. CB-214 and a motor carrier plate.

SALT SPRING ISLAND ARCHIVES

★ In the photo above, a fully loaded truck is displaying 1962 First Quarter plates (No. T137).

BOB DINGSDALE

★ One of the first acts of the reconvened Royal Commission was to introduce a quarterly licence that would be made available to truck loggers in 1961. No. T4-939 is an example of one of the first quarterly plates issued. Prior to this, it had only been possible to obtain annual licences.

by logging truck operators airing various and sundry grievances regarding the new fee structure and permitting regime.

As these hearings continued, it began to emerge that logging truck operators who decried the new fees as "exorbitant," were unable to demonstrate how this was so under cross-examination.[16] A rift also began to emerge within the trucking industry itself, between various logging industry groups that appeared before the commission, and urban truckers whose interests were ably represented by the Automotive Transport Association (ATA) of British Columbia. The ATA did not think logging truck operators should be entitled to a free ride on vehicle fees. Urban-based truckers felt that the services they provided were equally, if not more, important to the economic health of the province and were concerned that any concession granted to logging trucks would result in higher fees for all other commercial operators. The comparative absence of complaint from other components of the trucking industry seemed to indicate that the problem was specific to one aspect of forestry and not reflective of any inherent inequality contained within the new licensing fees. The ATA also felt that logging truck operators would benefit from a little education, and that the new fee structure should not "be jettisoned without trial merely to appease what the evidence suggests is a [small] minority group of users."[17]

Undeterred, logging truck operators continued to protest that their livelihood was in peril and that they were unable to bear any additional burdens. Even the quarterly licence plates introduced by the government came under criticism as being of little benefit unless the truck driver had the freedom to select the three-month quarter. This seeming ungratefulness led the commissioners to recommend that "the privilege of quarterly licences available to trucks carrying logs, poles and pilings should be terminated at the end of the current (1960) licensing year . . . [in order to] remove any appearance of favouritism or discrimination to a segment of truckers." The commissioners also recommended against the overweight permit, on the basis that if a road could handle a certain weight of vehicle it should be open.[18] The government would put aside the commissioners' recommendation to do away with the quarterly licences, and these would become a mainstay of the industry over the next 20 years. When the Province introduced staggered monthly registration to most other vehicle types in 1979, one of the principal benefits of the quarterly logging plates disappeared. Today, all commercial vehicle operators can register for a period of less than three months, and logging trucks are more likely to be seen with standard Commercial Truck plates (AA-0000) than quarterly T plates. Since 1989, somewhere around 35,000 of these quarterly plates have been issued, which is a drop in the bucket compared to the four million Commercial Truck plates that have been issued over the same period.

★ Although the "Beautiful British Columbia" slogan was first introduced to BC licence plates in 1964, it was 25 years before quarterly logging plates would sport the motto (and only after the series was restarted at T0-0000 in 1989 following the introduction of decaled renewals). The symbolic irony, of course, is that this occurred against a backdrop of increasing public opposition to the decidedly "un-Beautiful" practice of clear-cutting old-growth forests in the province (e.g., Meares Island in 1984 and Clayoquot Sound in 1993).

The Royal Commission was also charged with the task of reviewing "alternative methods of licence and permit fees . . . by means of reciprocal agreements with other Provinces and States." This meant that the provincial government was finally becoming interested in ways of reducing the barriers to commercially licensed trucks moving through other states and provinces. In the absence of reciprocity, BC truckers wishing to transport goods to sites within Washington, Oregon or even Alberta had to register in each of these jurisdictions, pay additional licence fees and attach an extra set of licence plates to the front of their cab. Over the previous 50 years, British Columbia had adhered to an essentially protectionist policy that limited competition among local operators to ensure service levels in remote and rural areas were maintained and that sufficient fees were collected from oversized vehicles. In fact, almost every other province and state had followed a similar path until the 1940s, when Washington and Oregon negotiated one of the first reciprocity agreements. This model would form the basis for the Uniform Vehicle Registration Proration and Reciprocity Agreement (also known as the "Western Compact"), which was created in 1955 and represented the first regional bloc of states to band together to reduce barriers to commercial vehicle movements.[19]

A more limited form of reciprocity had taken shape in Canada during this same period to improve the ability of "household-goods" movers to travel across provincial boundaries. All of the provinces, with the exception of British Columbia, were a party to this agreement. Consequently, British Columbia– based moving companies that wished to transport loads from Sidney, BC, to Sydney, Nova Scotia, had to register and display a licence plate from every province in order to travel from one end of the country to the other. The cost of registering in each province was estimated to be $2,613 per vehicle in 1958, whereas a similar mover based in Alberta would have only had to pay $959. If, however, British Columbia were to join this existing reciprocity agreement, the playing field became significantly more level as a moving company would only have to pay a single licence fee of $498, against the $521 licence fee that their Alberta competitor would have to pay. Yet, as British Columbia appeared unwilling to commit to reciprocity, a number of businesses had already begun

to relocate to other provinces where the cost of doing business was friendlier. The ATA believed that this was leading to "less work for local mechanics, less sales tax to the government and less business to local truck dealers and to the whole business community."[20]

The emergence of the Western Compact only further complicated matters for BC-based commercial truck operators, who now had to compete with two blocs of competitors who were not encumbered by the same licensing requirements and costs. Even more ominous, other states, such as Michigan, Wisconsin, Minnesota and North Dakota, were also exploring the formation of a reciprocity bloc. These states were very aware that despite having "some kind of agreement with most of the western provinces . . . none of them had any agreement with British Columbia."[21] By not participating in reciprocity agreements, regional travel patterns through the province were also being affected as commercial vehicles travelling between Alberta and Washington were increasingly opting to go through Montana rather than taking the shorter route and crossing at Kingsgate (where they faced additional licensing fees and had to display the necessary BC licence plates).[22]

The commissioners were convinced of the benefits to be received through negotiated reciprocity agreements and prorating licences and strongly encouraged the provincial government to seek entry to the Western Compact. The commissioners suggested limiting the issuance of 30-day permits to two per year, with a third trip triggering the need to obtain a full annual licence. Rather inexplicably, the provincial government implemented the commissioners' recommendation to limit the number of 30-day permits that would be issued in a year, but failed to enter into any reciprocal agreements with other jurisdictions. No longer able to obtain an unlimited number of permits, out-of-province operators removed their service to local cattle, fertilizer and other agricultural industries. For more rural parts of the province, the loss of this service resulted in financial hardship. Washington State further retaliated by similarly curtailing the number of permits it issued to BC-based trucks seeking to travel over its highway system. Consequently, BC trucking firms found themselves confronted with higher provincial licensing fees, no relaxation of the fees they paid in other jurisdictions and reduced access to Washington State.[23]

When the Royal Commission reconvened in 1960, the provincial government was urged to rethink its position and enter the Western Compact as overall revenues from out-of-province operators would likely increase; local operators would be able to compete in a broader market and potentially grow their business; and increased competition would lower costs to the benefit of the general public.[24] This time, the provincial government listened, and British Columbia formally entered the Western Compact on September 26, 1961.[25] To ensure compliance with the terms of the compact, as well as to allow for the easy identification of trucks that were operating under its terms, a new prorate licence plate type with a P prefix was issued starting in 1962.

While the removal of local restrictions and trade barriers through the negotiation of the Western Compact was beneficial for industry and consumer alike, the emergence of other regional blocs, such as the Multi-State

Agreement in the southeastern United States, did little to fully harmonize trucking regulations and licensing requirements. The regulatory differences between the Western Compact and the Multi-State Agreement were sometimes confusing, while the differing fees added to expenses incurred by the trucking industry. As the percentage of goods being moved by trucks continued to increase through the 1960s, these regional agreements became inadequate.[26] Work would begin in the late 1960s on a uniform set of rules, and in 1974 the International Registration Plan (IRP) was proclaimed, but with only eight member states.[27] The prospect of universal participation in the IRP seemed but a dream until the ratification of the North American Free Trade Agreement (NAFTA) in 1993. As part of NAFTA, the United States, Canada and Mexico tried to create a level playing field for trucking firms, with the help of the IRP.[28] The unique feature of IRP is that any vehicle classified as

★ Shown above is a rare example of a first-issue British Columbia prorate licence plate.

"apportionable" can operate either within or across jurisdictions with only a single licence plate and without the need for validating decals, spelling the end of the Bingo plate.[29] IRP specifically requires a participating jurisdiction to issue licence plates that contain the word "apportioned," or the abbreviations APP or PRP, and when British Columbia joined in 1996, the design of the province's prorate licence plate was modified accordingly.[30]

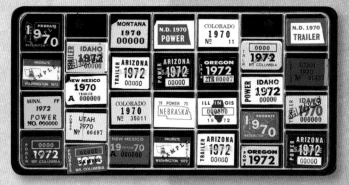

★ An example of a Bingo plate with early 1970s sample decals from BC and the other western states. IAN SLADE

The question of how to pay for a road system whose cost exceeded available funds was not confined solely to the provincial level. Unlike in other provinces, where a passable (if not always acceptable) percentage of the annual fees collected from driver's licences, fuel taxes and traffic fines was returned to municipalities to assist with road costs, the fees from these sources that were handed over to British Columbia municipalities in 1960 amounted to a

"trifling" 0.5 percent.[31] While always an option, the traditional use of property taxes to offset the costs of local road networks raised questions about the degree to which road users, especially heavy users who caused undue wear and tear, should be subsidized by the rest of the community. As a way out of this funding dilemma, an increasing number of municipalities had begun to turn to a section of the Municipal Act that allowed them to collect a licence fee from any person owning or keeping a vehicle for hire, or from the owner of a vehicle transporting goods within their municipality.[32] By the late 1950s, numerous municipalities, particularly those close to Vancouver and Victoria, were implementing bylaws requiring all commercial vehicles wanting to operate within their boundaries to contribute to the upkeep of the local road network through the purchase and display of municipally issued licence plates. For an operator whose territory happened to be the Fraser Valley, this potentially meant having to obtain licences from 28 separate "principalities" (as one trade association quipped), each of which required the payment of its own annual licence fee.[33]

C49·540
BRITISH COLUMBIA 60

★ In theory, the C prefix licence plates that had been created in 1936 granted a commercial vehicle operator the right to drive on all roads and streets in the province.

Equally irritating for commercial operators was the fact that no two municipalities were alike and they invariably had their own peculiar processes and regulations related to vehicle licensing.

Recognizing the increasing importance of the commercial trucking industry to the provincial economy and seeking to protect it from local interference, the provincial government had enacted the Motor Carrier Act in 1939. Unfortunately, the drafters of this legislation failed to foresee that a commercial vehicle would invariably have to exit the highway system in order

★ While the Municipal Act allowed a municipality to collect a licence fee from any person owning or keeping a vehicle for hire—or from the owner of a vehicle transporting goods within a municipality—a quirk of the legislation specified that a municipality choosing to enact such a levy could only do so for six-month intervals. Consequently, the majority of municipal licence plates issued prior to 1963 denote the year of issue as well as either "1st HALF" (being from January 1 to June 30) or "2nd HALF" (being from July 1 to December 31).[37]

to either receive or deliver its freight. This meant that once a commercial vehicle began travelling upon a municipally maintained road, it lost all of its protections under the Motor Carrier Act and had to comply with the relevant local bylaws.[34]

★ The prefix of a motor carrier licence plate signified the use of that particular vehicle, whether it be for the public or private movement of goods or people. Although variations of these plates had been issued since the mid-1920s, when the Province introduced a new Motor Carrier Act in 1939 it was intended to prevent municipalities from meddling in what was becoming the increasingly important transportation of people and goods by motor vehicle.

Although this perceived loophole had not been raised as an issue of concern during the Royal Commission's first series of hearings, it became more pronounced during the second round of hearings in 1960.[35] Municipalities were accused of using their authority to pass commercial vehicle bylaws as a

way to create "trade barriers" to shield local businesses from competition.[36] A Saanich bylaw that was struck down by the courts in 1959 was held up as an example after a local reeve admitted that it

A Licence to Make Housecalls

Medical doctors were among the first professionals to avail themselves of the mobility offered by automobiles when making house calls or responding to emergencies. In some communities, the local doctor was issued with a special identifier that allowed him to freely park anywhere in town or to exceed posted speed limits. In 1938, the MVB standardized this practice with the introduction of special PN prefix plates to medical doctors, but discontinued the practice six years later as a "Dope Precaution" at the request of doctors who were tired of continually being subjected to "holdups and burglaries" by addicts able to identify them by their licence plates.[38]

★ In Penticton, the local doctor, R.B. White, displayed a name plate on the back of his vehicle that allowed certain privileges within the city when conducting medical business. **COURTESY OF PENTICTON MUSEUM & ARCHIVES**

had been adopted following "reports of trucks from up-Island operating in the municipality." In retaliation, other municipalities began to pass similar bylaws, not as a way to raise funds to maintain the road network, but as a weapon against the "trade barriers" imposed by others. In response, commercial vehicle operators began to licence their vehicles only in municipalities where they did the majority of their business as a way to ensure that they would earn back any investment in a municipal licence. Operators of larger fleets would licence one vehicle for a certain set of municipalities and another vehicle for a different set of municipalities; however, if one of these vehicles happened to be out when an order was received for the municipality it was licensed to operate in, the shipment would have to wait until the vehicle returned to the yard. Not only did this situation create inefficiencies within the transportation system, but it stifled competition and inflated rates as truckers began to refuse orders rather than purchase a licence or run the risk of operating in violation of a municipal bylaw.[39]

The Royal Commission did not mince words when describing the effects that municipal bylaws regulating commercial vehicle operators were having on the economy of the province:

> *The pyramiding effect of these levies by many municipalities on commercial vehicles . . . is as effective a barrier to inter-provincial commercial road transport as municipal embargos or tariff-walls—which are illegal. Efficient and competitive intra-provincial commercial road transport is seriously endangered by the "jungle" of multiple municipal commercial vehicle levies.[40]*

The commissioners refrained from making a specific recommendation on the matter of municipal licensing, but they did suggest that municipal fees should be capped and the loophole in the Motor Carrier Act closed. If these steps were taken, "separate regulatory or right-to-use [municipal] vehicle licence plates should no longer be needed."

In order to allow municipalities to respond to the charges that had been levelled against them, a legislative committee convened hearings into the matter of municipal licence plates in early 1962. Representing the interests of local governments, the Union of British Columbia Municipalities (UBCM) adopted, rather shrewdly, the very argument used by the provincial government when it established the Royal Commission. Namely, what was fair at the provincial level was no less fair at the local level, and heavy users of municipal  infrastructure—such as roads—should be expected to contribute to its upkeep. Moreover, the municipal licensing of commercial vehicles was an effective method for the recovery of road costs, while the ability to regulate the nature of businesses being carried

on within a municipal boundary was the natural right of any community. In 1961, Surrey had licensed approximately 169 commercial vehicles belonging to local businesses versus 499 commercial vehicles that originated outside of its boundaries. If the ability to require licences of these vehicles were removed, Surrey would be deprived of an important source of revenue, while non-local businesses would reap the benefit of local taxpayers now having to maintain the local road network. Some municipalities recognized that the existing system was not perfect and supported some minor modifications, including a licensing year that coincided with that of the Province (March 1 to February 28); a consistent fee across municipalities; the ability to license all commercial vehicles (not just those engaged in delivery and collection); and centralized collection and reimbursement of fees on a per capita basis.[41]

Given that a majority of road-user charges were already collected via taxes and charges administered by the Province, and economists were increasingly advocating that responsibility for road-user charges be centralized at the provincial level, the recommendations of the legislative committee were somewhat predictable.[42] For the 1963 licensing year, the creation of a single uniform municipal licence plate was recommended, with all licensing fees to be collected by the Department of Municipal Affairs (which would then disburse the fees on a per capita basis to participating municipalities). This new licence plate would allow a vehicle to operate anywhere in the province.[43]

★ An unidentified individual purchases a 1963 municipal licence plate from the Licence Bureau at the City of Vancouver. Fortunately, he was able to obtain his licence plate and pose for a picture without the need to extinguish his cigarette. *VANCOUVER PROVINCE* PHOTO. VANCOUVER PUBLIC LIBRARY 41148

In 1987, administration of the Commercial Vehicle Licence (CVL) Program was transferred to the UBCM, and licence plates were replaced with a decal to be attached to the windshield of a vehicle.

After 50 years, the future of the CVL Program remains uncertain as the fees that are collected on a yearly basis and distributed to municipalities are almost inconsequential in terms of funding the existing road system. Industry groups such as the BC Trucking Association (BCTA) are advocating for its abolition on the basis that "the benefits once provided to commercial vehicles within a municipality (for example, commercial loading zones) have been greatly reduced or else are virtually non-existent." Local governments' attitudes towards the licensing program also vary, as some sporadically enforce the requirement to display a licence decal, while others do not appear to enforce it at all. This creates confusion among commercial operators whenever their vehicles are ticketed, especially larger for-hire and private fleets, which often operate across municipal and provincial boundaries.[44] Despite this apparent lackadaisical approach to the CVL Program, a number of Lower Mainland municipalities have slowly begun to re-create some of the same barriers to inter-municipal vehicle movements that led to provincial regulation in the 1960s, especially with regard to the taxi industry (which will be discussed in the next chapter).

2000
COMMERCIAL VEHICLE
LICENCE PLATE
38325
B.C.

2001
COMMERCIAL VEHICLE
LICENCE DECAL
54000
B.C.

★ Despite the Commercial Vehicle Licence Program being transferred to the UBCM, followed by the replacement of the licence plates with a windshield decal in 1987, the Municipal Act was never amended to reflect these changes. Consequently, and in order to ensure consistency with the act, the decals issued from 1987 to 2000 included wording identifying them as "licence plates." Only following the introduction of a new Local Government Act in 2000 would the definition of "licence plate" be amended to include a "licence decal."
UNION OF BC MUNICIPALITIES

In the
INTERESTS of the
TRAVELLING PUBLIC

7

If someone at the turn of the 20th century wanted to travel or transport freight over land, the only practical option was rail. Railways were so dominant that governments in Canada and the United States began to regulate their operation in the mid-1800s to protect farmers and other businesses from the railways' monopolistic tendencies. The most common measure was rate controls, which limited the maximum fee a railway could charge to move freight. The Crow Rate, which was imposed on the Canadian Pacific Railway for the benefit of Prairie grain farmers, is probably the best-known example in Western Canada. Minimum-rate controls were also implemented to ensure railway companies did not engage in ruinous competition to the detriment of the broader economy.[1] While these regulations generally achieved their objectives, they also created a straitjacket that would make it very difficult for the railways to respond to new competitors. When the first trucks appeared on the streets of major urban centres such as Vancouver after 1900, they were not considered a threat to railways as most were used as drayage vehicles to haul freight over short distances to or from a railway yard.[2] Poor road networks throughout North America also made it impractical to transport goods any farther than a few kilometres by truck.

By 1922, the Dominion Bureau of Statistics was reporting that "the automotive transport industry is just beginning to be a factor in the transportation of passengers and freight in this country . . . and commercial trucks are being used in greater numbers to carry lighter shipments of property between some of the larger centres served by adequately surfaced highways."[3] Two technological innovations would fundamentally alter the competitive balance between locomotives and trucks in the early 1920s. One was the creation of a heavy-duty chassis that made hauling freight by truck more feasible, while the other involved the development of a fifth wheel with kingpin trailer-coupling device that enabled one truck to deliver and receive multiple trailers in a single trip.[4] Initially, the railways were quite prepared to cede some of their less profitable branch lines to truck transporters, who quickly displaced short-haul steam and electric railways. Truckers were quick to take advantage of the emerging provincial highway system, the cost of which was largely subsidized by the general taxpayer and private passenger vehicle. Truckers also exploited the rate structure used by the railways, which relied on overcharging on manufactured and high-end commodities in order to subsidize the cost of bulk and low-value commodities. As these rates

★ One of the earliest known examples of a licence plate issued by a BC municipality is this 1912 "Express & Dray" from the City of Vancouver.

★ A one-ton Studebaker owned by D.N. McConnell carrying load of Leckie Boots (1918).

CITY OF VANCOUVER ARCHIVES, CVA 99-5158, STUART THOMSON

bore no relationship to the actual costs of transportation, the truck operator could undercut the railways on high-end shipments. Delivering an item by truck was also proving to be quicker, as the railways had to first switch goods from the rail car to a drayage vehicle at the local yard.[5]

In an attempt to stem the loss of traffic from their lines, the railways lobbied for the institution of trucking regulations similar to those that governed their industry. Pennsylvania became the first state to adopt trucking regulations in 1914, with an additional 35 states following by 1925. During the Depression, even some trucking firms came to favour government regulation. As the railway companies had already discovered, the barriers to entry in the commercial freight industry were becoming very low. As economic conditions worsened, many large, well-established trucking firms found their businesses threatened by fly-by-night operators who offered cut-rate prices that ultimately forced down wages and disrupted the whole rate structure in an area. For established operators, one of the best ways to combat this was to create barriers that would make it difficult for someone to hang out their shingle, proclaim themselves a freight hauler and charge whatever rates they felt like. In British Columbia, the economic regulation of the trucking industry occurred for many of the same reasons as elsewhere in North America.[6]

As trucks were reshaping the commercial freight industry, taxis and buses were challenging the supremacy of the horse and carriage and streetcar in the movement of passen-

104. White Steamer, owned by Wm. Hayward, of Commercial Hotel. First car for hire in Vancouver Driver:- H.E. Campbell, next archbishop Dontonville Father Le Chesne (in hat)

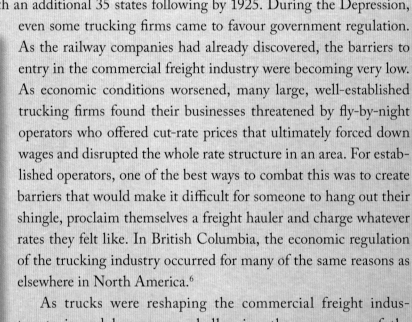

★ In 1904, this White Steamer, owned by William Hayward of Commercial Drive, was purported to be the first taxi (or "vehicle for hire") to operate within the City of Vancouver.

Although not clearly visible in this particular photo, Mr. Hayward's White Steamer was issued registration No. 7 on May 5, 1904. **CITY OF VANCOUVER ARCHIVES, TRANS P15.2, JAMES MATTHEWS**

gers within and between urban centres. For-hire private vehicles soon provided a quicker, more flexible service than established streetcar lines. The competition between these modes of transportation led to concerns about the safety and reliability of the vehicles and their drivers. Intense competition was thought to encourage drivers to cut corners by reducing their rates to unsustainable levels, working longer hours and performing less maintenance on their vehicles. Left unchecked, this unbridled competition could jeopardize public safety and lead all of those operating within a specific area to economic ruin. If private business then concluded that there was no money to be made on a particular route, it might be abandoned, to the detriment of the community.

★ Taxi cabs competing with electric streetcars on Granville Street (circa 1915).
CITY OF VANCOUVER ARCHIVES, TRANS N87.11, WILLIAM STARK

★ The concern for public safety was not unfounded. In this incident, a taxi slid over the Georgia Street viaduct on March 15, 1931, after attempting to avoid construction. The driver, Ernest "Safety First Ernie" Burchell, along with three passengers died as a result of the 48 foot fall.[7]
CITY OF VANCOUVER ARCHIVES, CVA 99-2526, STUART THOMSON

★ The occasional perils of private transport by bus in the 1940s. Space is limited and the seating is less than secure as a driver helps a passenger into the back of his McDonald Bus Line vehicle (a Renfrew Bus Line vehicle is pictured at left).
CITY OF VANCOUVER ARCHIVES, CVA 1184-2630, JACK LINDSEY

★ No one knows for exactly what purpose the 1927 Special Permit licence plate was issued, but since it does bear the initials of the Public Works Department ("P.W.D."), it is thought to be related to motor carrier regulation. The 1930 and 1934 plates are more common examples of permits issued for the movement of people (1930) and freight (1934).

By the mid-1930s, most of the provinces were limiting the number of taxi and bus operators who could work on any one route to ensure a certain level of service was provided. The "public interest" would be used to justify the protection of existing taxi and bus operators against new competitors and to ensure that minimum safety standards were met when passengers were being transported.[8]

Since 1925, any vehicle being used to transport passengers or freight had to submit a route schedule and insurance to the provincial government, after which a formal Certificate of Approval had to be obtained from the Minister of Public Works. This process was amended in 1930 when the licensing requirements for passenger and freight vehicles were separated, and was eventually extended to virtually all forms of passenger and freight transportation in 1935 in an attempt to deal with the disruptive practices of fly-by-night operators during the Depression. Under this new regulatory regime, the movement of passengers or freight, whether for compensation or private purposes, required the formal approval of the ministry. The complexity of this system can be seen in the number of different vehicle classifications—11 in total—and corresponding letter prefixes that were created for use on the new Carrier Licence (CL) plates.

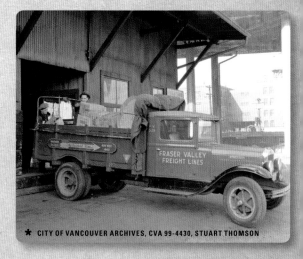

★ CITY OF VANCOUVER ARCHIVES, CVA 99-4430, STUART THOMSON

Difficulties associated with administering the legislation led the government to introduce the Motor Carrier Act in 1940 and transfer the day-to-day management of motor carriers from the Public Works Department to the

Public Utilities Commission (PUC), which, in turn, established the Motor Carrier Commission (MCC) that same year. To appreciate how pervasive the regulation of commercial vehicles had become under the MCC, one only need look at the hurdles a farmer now faced in bringing produce to market. In order to transport agricultural, orchard or dairy products produced on their farm and in their own truck, farmers had to receive the approval of the Public Works Department and affix a K prefix plate to the truck. Without this approval, the only option would be to contract with someone who was licensed by the department and have that person deliver the products, at a cost, to the wholesaler or packing house.

The tide of regulation only began to ebb in the 1950s. The thicket of rules and regulations that taxi, bus and truck operators had to navigate when travelling between jurisdictions had begun to impede economic progress. In 1951, the federal Royal Commission on Transportation found that freight movement by truck was in direct competition with the railways, and truckers were operating inter-provincially and, in some instances, internationally—which brought the industry under federal jurisdiction. In order to better "co-ordinate and harmonize the operations of trucks," the Royal Commission concluded that there was a "public interest" in having federal regulations extended to this industry. The Supreme Court also found that the federal government had jurisdiction over inter-provincial commercial passenger transportation. At issue had been the New Brunswick Motor Carrier Board's refusal of an application from a bus company operating between Boston, Massachusetts, and various points in Nova Scotia to pick up and drop off passengers within the province. The Supreme Court concluded that it was not within New Brunswick's legislative powers to prohibit the company from delivering passengers into or out of the province.[9] To provide clarity to the industry, the federal government

★ "Mystery Trip" indeed, as this poor fellow is left scratching his head over his intended destination. Fortunately, he has the necessary plates to take his riders wherever they are going. Below the 1953 Commercial licence plate (No. C70-220) is Motor Carrier plate No. A 47, denoting a "Public Passenger Vehicle" (i.e., a bus). Only 96 A carrier plates were issued in 1953. ART JONES PHOTO, VANCOUVER PUBLIC LIBRARY 41157

* 1957 was the last year that motorists seeking to use their own vehicles to transport their own goods would be required to obtain a licence from the Motor Carrier Commission and display either a K or an L prefix plate.

assumed responsibility for the regulation of inter-provincial motor carriers in 1954, but chose to delegate the regulatory authority back to the provinces, as they retained the expertise and the infrastructure to properly manage the industry.[10] In exchange, the provinces were expected to work towards the harmonization of regulations throughout the country and reduce barriers to the inter-provincial movement of commercial vehicles. In British Columbia, the requirement that farmers and others seeking to use their own vehicles to move freight must obtain motor carrier plates was phased out after 1957. Thanks to this one change, the total number of vehicles required to be licensed by the Motor Carrier Commission declined by almost 75 percent between 1957 and 1958.[11]

* A rather busy plate with almost too much information on it was introduced in 1970. For whatever reason, the Public Utilities Commission was using the plate as a way to promote its regulation of motor carriers.

In April 1973, the newly elected NDP government abolished the Public Utilities Commission and transferred authority for motor carriers to a newly created Motor Carrier Commission, commencing with the 1974 licensing year.

This is considered to have resulted in the rather slap-happy change to the 1974 plates that saw the bottom quarter of the plate cut off where, it is assumed, the words "Public Utilities Commission" had already been stamped.

By the 1980s, the Motor Carrier Commission's mandate was increasingly at odds with the direction being taken by the provincial and federal governments towards deregulation of key sectors of the economy such as energy, communications, finance and transportation. In 1987, the federal government began to reclaim the territory it had ceded to the provinces in the 1950s and implemented legislative changes that limited the ability of provincial motor carrier regulators to restrict commercial truck drivers operating across provincial boundaries.[12] This struck at the "public interest" test that the MCC

Ham Radio Licence Plates

The Motor Carrier Commission wasn't the only agency to issue licence plates that played an important public safety role. When the Fraser River flooded in 1948, 16,000 people were evacuated from the Upper Fraser Valley; 2,300 homes were destroyed or damaged; and all rail, road and air connections to the east were severed. Lacking any special markings, amateur ("ham") radio operators with mobile equipment in their cars were turned away by police and other authorities at the flood zone, unable to get to their allotted positions and aid in the rescue operations. For years afterwards, Stanley Carnell, the MLA for Peace River and a ham operator himself, lobbied the legislature every spring during the period of licence plate renewals for a special ham plate. Only belatedly, after every other Canadian province and 46 of 50 states had the plates, did BC institute its own in 1963.

★ Identifiable by its first three letters of VE7 or VA7, these licence plates are designed to ensure that amateur radio operators are easily recognized in the event of a natural disaster and able to assist with emergency communications.

★ DAVE MARSHALL

By the mid-1990s, the number of two-letter suffixes available to operators was becoming scarce. Nanaimo-based operator Dave Marshall recalls, "When I aspired to become a ham operator in the early '90s, it was considered desirable to have a two-letter suffix after the VE7 (e.g., VE7DD) as part of your call sign—these were usually unavailable and assigned only to long time amateurs. With that in mind and only being a beginner, I was able to get a two-letter call sign in the form of VE7TWO." In 1999, a new VA7 prefix was created to accommodate the growing number of ham radio operators in the province as well as those who felt that all the good suffixes under the VE7 prefix had already been taken.[13]

★ 1999 marked the last year that commercial freight vehicles were required to be licensed under the Motor Carrier Act and display a separate carrier licence plate.

had been using for decades to fulfill its mandate of fostering sound economic conditions in the transportation business. Under this policy, all applicants seeking a licence had to prove that there was a public need for their service and demonstrate how the public interest would be affected. Prior to approving an application, the MCC would also invite existing licence holders to express their own views on where the public interest might lie. Not surprisingly, established operators would routinely use these opportunities to object to the granting of any new licences in the belief that increased competition would adversely affect their livelihoods.[14] Many seeking to enter the industry came to see the commission as acting in the interests of established licence holders to the detriment of new competitors and the travelling public. The federal government tried to eliminate this bias in the commercial freight sector by introducing a "reverse onus" public interest test for new inter-provincial licences. Within a few years of the passage of NAFTA, the commercial freight industry was completely deregulated, and motor carrier licence plates for most freight vehicles were phased out by 1999.[15]

Whereas deregulation was being encouraged in the commercial trucking industry to improve service and pricing, consolidation in the taxi industry was seen by the Motor Carrier Commission as a challenge to its mandate of ensuring that both public service and safety were fairly and effectively provided.[16] For decades, small, family-run companies had operated taxis, but intense competition within the industry, especially in Vancouver and Victoria had begun to change this in the late 1980s.

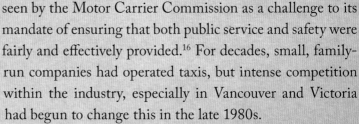

★ The Vet's Taxi Service, which operated in Penticton after the war, is typical of the smaller, family-run taxi companies that existed throughout the province prior to the 1980s. PHOTO BY JACK STOCKS, COURTESY OKANAGAN ARCHIVE TRUST SOCIETY WWW.OLDPHOTOS.CA

Fare Play The changing nature of the taxi industry at this time was underscored by a 1992 application by Empress Taxi of Victoria for an additional nine motor carrier licence plates. Empress was accused by its competitors of improperly switching plates between vehicles (including from buses to taxis), of selling or renting plates to third-party operators and of attempting to drive independent operators out of business by overpaying for the rights to "prime taxi sites."

Other taxicab operators within the city, including the Greater Victoria Taxi Owners' Association, were concerned that Empress's business model of requiring its drivers to pay a flat $200-per-week fee—which bore no relation to revenues generated—was forcing some drivers to borrow money in order to meet their lease obligations. This raised the age-old spectre of rate cutting, drivers working longer hours, questionable vehicle maintenance levels and declining financial stability for others attempting to operate within the Victoria area.

The commission ultimately refused the application and fined Empress for its actions in relation to the leasing and use of expired motor carrier licence plates.[17]

★ An example of a 1991 motor carrier licence plate, the same type that Empress Taxi of Victoria was accused of swapping between vehicles and leasing to third parties.

Continued problems within the industry led the provincial government to appoint a Taxi Study Panel chaired by Stan Lanyon, QC. The panel found that most taxi companies were now operating under a shareholder structure in which a company owned the fleet licence (with its designated number of plates) and ran the dispatch service, but vehicles were generally owned by individual operators who were also the shareholders of the company. Taxi drivers generally had to purchase a half-share in one of these companies, which entitled them to operate a vehicle during either the night or day shift. Trading shares in these companies in order to obtain the motor carrier licence plate was legally questionable and not recognized by the commission. Nevertheless, private markets in the Vancouver and Victoria areas soon became an indispensible facet of the industry. In the Lower Mainland, the price of these shares could be anywhere from $30,000 in an outlying area to as much as $160,000 for a half-share in the restricted Vancouver market (by 2010, this price had skyrocketed to over $500,000). This unique aspect of the industry—the incredibly high cost of entry combined with the low profitability of operating a taxi—led Lanyon to conclude that incentives to cut corners were pervasive:

> Drivers have no vested interest in either the mechanical condition of their vehicles or the financial success of the company. Shareholders have no way of knowing if drivers are accurately reporting their income, and have no incentive for rewarding drivers for improved service or skill levels . . . The low entry-level standards for drivers ensures that there is always an abundant supply of drivers willing to replace those who might complain of their treatment. The result paradoxically is an industry that is both over and under-regulated – a situation that ill serves those within the industry and compromises the quality of service to the general public.[18]

When the newly elected BC Liberal Party began to implement its "New Era" platform of reduced government regulation and bureaucratic red tape following the 2001 provincial election, the Motor Carrier Commission became a natural target. Continued regulation of the commercial passenger transportation sector was anachronistic to the new administration. Yet the Liberals had enjoyed strong support in ridings around East Vancouver and Surrey, which were home to taxi drivers heavily invested in their motor carrier licences. The government ultimately introduced a new Passenger Transportation Act in 2004, which continued the regulation of the taxi and private bus industries. The new legislation also responded to concerns expressed by the taxi industry regarding the age-old problem of rogue operators.[19] A new Passenger Transportation Board was created and continues to make decisions about allowing new entrants into the industry based on the perceived "public need," whether an applicant is deemed "fit and proper" (i.e., has that person participated in any unlawful activity or declared bankruptcy?), and the overall effect of additional competition on the viability of other operators.[20] Licensees are now required to affix a rather gaudy supplementary plate to the front of their vehicle to show that they are properly authorized to transport passengers.

Many Lower Mainland municipalities also impose their own limits on the number of taxis that can operate within their boundaries and impose their own set of licensing and registration fees. Before someone can apply to the Passenger Transportation Board for a licence to operate within Vancouver, he or she must obtain a Vehicle for Hire licence from the City. In 2007, it was estimated that over the preceding 17 years, only 33 taxis had been added to the city's fleets, despite a 65 percent increase in passengers arriving at Vancouver International Airport and a nearly 100 percent increase in visitors arriving by cruise ship.[21] If the creep of

★ SCOTT ROBARTS

★ On June 24, 2004, the Passenger Transportation Act came into effect, replacing the Motor Carrier Act. Licence holders were given until February 28, 2005, to "convert" their licences, which would from then on display the provincial flag and a serial number starting with 8. These licence plates are manufactured by Astrographic.

★ The licensing requirements for taxis and private buses demand the display of the appropriate provincial licence plate(s): a Passenger Carrier plate as well as a Vehicle for Hire plate when operating within the City of Vancouver. In this instance, one can tell from the apportioned licence plate that this is a private tour bus that serves the City of Vancouver and crosses provincial boundaries in the process. MARK REES

anti-competitive municipal regulation continues, the province will likely have to consider expanding the scope of the Passenger Carrier plates—in much the same way it did with the municipal licence plates in the early 1960s—to provide operators with the ability to cross municipal boundaries without fear of penalty.

8 The WORLD'S OLDEST LICENCE PLATE?

It is not often that one of the great questions of licence plate collecting is answered, but that is precisely what appeared to happen on October 19, 2010, when the *Victoria Times Colonist* newspaper published various headlines proclaiming Victoria the "birthplace of the licence plate" and home to the "world's oldest licence plate."[1] The occasion that these headlines were marking was the awarding of a Guinness World Record to local collector John Roberts in recognition of his claim that a "licence plate" from his collection had originally been issued by the City of Victoria to a hackney carriage in 1884. As mentioned in Chapter 1, the commonly accepted "first" automobile licence plate was issued by the City of Paris in 1893, so this meant the City of Victoria licence plate was, in the estimation of Guinness World Records, the oldest known to exist. However, many local collectors, including me, have always believed that these City of Victoria plates were issued in 1913. What was even more surprising was how far the idea that this could be the world's oldest licence plate had progressed without anyone questioning the validity of the claim.

★ Esquimalt resident John Roberts with the No. 6 City of Victoria licence plate and the certificate from Guinness World Records Ltd. confirming it to be "the oldest licence plate" (2010).
ADRIAN LAM OF THE *VICTORIA TIMES COLONIST*

★ Dan Christian (above, in 2012) with the two 1913 BC passenger plates acquired by his father in the 1950s along with the a porcelain "driver's licence" (above, right). JOHN ROBERTS ("DRIVER'S LICENCE" IMAGE)

The seeds of this tale were planted in early 2006 when Victoria resident Dan Christian, a retired appraiser, began to investigate the potential value of three porcelain plates his father had acquired decades earlier. Wrapped together and stored in his basement for years, the stash comprised two first-issue provincial plates from 1913, along with a No. 6 City of Victoria licence plate that was sandwiched between the other two. Christian was advised by Joe Armitage, a local plate collector, as well as other knowledgeable fellows in the Lower Mainland that 1913 BC licence plates are relatively common and might be worth a couple of hundred dollars each, depending on their condition. The City of Victoria plate, however, was significantly rarer, with only five similar plates known to exist at that time, none of which were single digit. When the No. 168 City of Victoria plate was listed on an Internet auction site a few years earlier, it sold for over 1,000 USD. Given the condition of Christian's plate, it was not inconceivable that it could be sold for a similar price, if not more.

Word of this new "find" soon began to circulate within the small community of BC collectors, but Christian was in no rush to part with the plates. Finally, on the evening of June 30, 2008, Esquimalt resident John Roberts made Christian an offer for the No. 6 plate and an accompanying porcelain driver's licence badge. Christian accepted, believing he had done pretty well on the deal.[2]

Little was known about these plates at the time, and even the City itself had lost track of their original purpose. In 1964, 11-year-old Teddy Gorse and his friend, 10-year-old David Harris, went on a mission to determine the history of the No. 89 City of Victoria plate that Teddy's father, George, had unearthed while digging in the backyard of their Brooke Street property (near the Ross Bay Cemetery). The boys brought the plate to the staff at City Hall, who were stumped as to its origins and "thought the licence might have been used for a horse and buggy transfer firm." The owner of No. 98, Joe Howroyd, had uncovered his plate in similar circumstances when plowing his Gordon Head farm in the 1950s. Howroyd displayed the plate on the wall of a hangar at the Butler-Howroyd Airstrip in Saanichton in the hopes that someone might be able to offer additional insights. Unfortunately for Gorse and Harris, Howroyd was unable to shed any light on the matter, advising them that "no one who has seen it has volunteered any information" about its origins.[3]

Nevertheless, the plates themselves do provide a number of fairly significant clues as to their origin and purpose, which is what led many collectors to conclude that they had likely been issued in 1913. The first clue is the porcelain, which was first used on licence plates in 1903 after the Commonwealth of Massachusetts and City of Philadelphia issued standardized licence plate series that year.

If there has been a recurring theme throughout the history of BC licence plates, it is that innovation and changes in design, issuance or manufacturing rarely happen in isolation. Then, as now, issuing authorities routinely communicated with each other (they even have their own association), and advise on trends and practices in their jurisdictions. According to Eric Taylor, an authority on the use of porcelain licence plates:

> When the application of porcelain to license plates was first made in 1903, the floodgates immediately opened. The City of St. Louis began issuing porcelains in 1904 and by 1905, every state in New England was using them . . . With each successive year, more and more states, provinces and local municipalities across North America adopted porcelain license plates.[4]

Over the next two decades, approximately 1,500 varieties of porcelain licence plates were issued throughout North America, with the peak use of the material occurring between 1910 and 1915. There was also an uncanny resemblance between the City's licence plates and those manufactured for the province by McClary for use on motorcycles in 1913. The porcelain coating on a heavy-gauge steel base is the same, as are the dimensions of the two plates. The

★ While the No. 98 plate that Joe Howroyd unearthed in the 1950s remains unaccounted for, the No. 89 plate George Gorse found in 1964 eventually made its way into the hands of collectors. **ALAN BETTS**

★ Shown (above) is an example of the 1903 porcelain licence plate issued by Massachusetts along with a 1903 plate issued by the City of Philadelphia (below). These and other early examples of porcelain licence plates generally display a very basic layout comprising two colours and the absence of any intricate designs. **ERIC TAYLOR**

★ The similarities between the City of Victoria plate and the first motorcycle plate issued by the Province in 1913 are readily apparent in this photo.

ERIC TAYLOR

bolthole placement and rivets in each corner, as well as the slots along the tops of the plates, all correspond as does the vertical alignment of the two lines running through the plates. If the City's plates were not issued in 1913, it seemed certain that they were a product of the golden age of porcelain.

The first hint that this assumption was about to be challenged appeared in an article entitled "World's Oldest Licence Plates" published by the Victoria-based *Senior Living Magazine* in March 2010. Without verifying the assertion, the publication announced: "Victoria is the true pioneer of the North American licence plate," adding that a claim for "bragging rights to Victoria as the birthplace of the licence plate has now been forwarded to 'Guinness Book of World Records.'" The basis of this claim was an obscure city bylaw that was adopted in 1883 to improve the conduct of hackney carriage drivers plying city streets. Starting on January 1 of the following year, all hackney carriages would need to be registered with the City and display "two badges," one on the inside of the vehicle and the other on the outside. This was intended to facilitate the identification of drivers whose conduct was deemed unbecoming (due to drunkenness or foul language) or who were charging exorbitant fares (principally to visiting tourists). Serial offenders would have their licences revoked by the City.[5] The claim to being the "birthplace of the licence plate" rested on the reference to the "two badges" in the bylaw and a belief that this described the white-and-black No. 6 plate and driver's licence No. 238.

For Pender Island resident Pierre Delacôte, the suggestion that the No. 6 plate could be the "world's oldest" was simply untrue. Ten years earlier, Delacôte had placed an advertisement in an online bulletin board seeking old licence plates. One of the responses came from a fellow in Oregon who was curious about the origins of a little black-and-white porcelain licence plate from the City of Victoria. In describing the plate to Delacôte, he also happened to mention that the number on the plate was 1. The owner of the plate, Bob Reeve, was unwilling to part with it, but did agree to send Delacôte a photo. A well-timed road trip south of the border in May 2010 allowed Delacôte to finally see this plate for himself, obtain some better photos, and discover more of its history. As it turns out, the plate had originally come from Bill Salt, whose grandfather, Samuel Eastman, had operated a hack stand on Yates Street, just a few blocks from the Empress Hotel in Victoria's Inner Harbour. Eastman first appeared in the city directory as a "hack" in 1909, was trading as a "Hack and Cab" company in 1916 and was the last hack business in the city two short years later (after which the last of the horses was replaced by an automobile). During his career as a hack, Eastman prepared special carriages that carried President T. Roosevelt and Irish tenor John McCormack. After driving the streets of Victoria for over 50 years, Eastman retired in 1940. The family would sell his estate after his death in 1945—including the horse carriages—but retained the No. 1 plate as a memento left to hang in the garage of their Saanich home over the years. Rather tellingly, in 1884, Samuel Eastman would have been only 12 years old and unlikely to have been working as a hack, let alone be issued with the first registration number.[6]

★ Pierre Delacôte with the highly desirable City of Victoria No. 1 licence plate (May 2010).
PIERRE DELACÔTE

While researching this book in 2010, I planned a trip from the Okanagan to Vancouver Island to visit the various libraries and archives located in Victoria. On the last night of research, which I spent at the law library at the University of Victoria, I came across a volume of city bylaws. Playing a hunch, I checked the listing of bylaws passed between 1900 and 1914 and solved my questions about the origin and purpose of the City's porcelain licence plates. Yes, the City had passed a bylaw in 1883 to regulate hackney carriages, but this had been replaced by a new Hired Vehicles Bylaw in 1901. This newer bylaw did away with the need to display a badge on the interior and exterior of a vehicle with the requirement for only a single "metallic badge bearing the number under

which such vehicle is registered" on the exterior (see left). This requirement for a badge was amended again in 1912 when hired vehicles—which now included automobiles—were henceforward required to display . . . (drum roll) . . . "a white enamelled plate of a size not less than six by four inches, exhibiting said number in blue or black figures not less than three inches in height and the City Coat of Arms above said number."[7] Not coincidentally, the dimensions of the No. 6 plate and others like it are approximately eight by five inches, with the numbers exactly three inches in height. The 1912 amendments also required the drivers of these vehicles to carry an "elliptical metal enamelled badge 2½ inches in diameter, and the letters shall be not less than 3–4 inches in height." What is especially interesting is how this wording sounds much like a purchase order. As noted in Chapter 2, McClary was not the most creative outfit when it came to designing licence plates, and the bylaw's reference to either a blue or black colour seems to suggest that the City did not yet know which of McClary's two basic designs it would be receiving.

The correspondence of Superintendent of Provincial Police Colin Campbell contains another interesting observation on licence plate use in this period. Writing to the California Secretary of State on June 18, 1913, Campbell advised that he was finding "many automobile owners complain that [the plates] chip very easily and become disfigured." Before making a decision on whether to use porcelain again in 1914, Campbell was "making some enquiries as to the material used in other places and the satisfaction it has given," and was curious as to the type of material used in California and if it was worth considering for BC.[8] Had the City been using porcelain licence plates over the previous three decades, this issue of chipping and disfiguration would surely not have come as a surprise to the superintendent—who also happened to be a resident of Victoria. Unfortunately, this information only came to light after Guinness World Records had certified the No. 6 plate to be the "world's oldest."

In the days after the announcement, other licence plate collectors immediately contested the claim, while a number of interesting revelations began to surface. Why, some asked, had dozens of other jurisdictions followed the lead of Philadelphia and Massachusetts in issuing porcelain licence plates after 1903, but had not followed the path purportedly blazed by Victoria 20 years earlier? Had the Victoria plates been such a catastrophic failure that enamelling plants refused to accept any more licence plate contracts for the next two decades? How, 18 years before Dr. Hart drove the first car down Johnson Street, had the City and the plate manufacturer been able to foresee the proper placement of boltholes, thereby allowing these plates to be easily fitted on automobiles?[9]

In attempting to verify his claim, Roberts had contacted other prominent collectors across North America earlier in 2010, asking if anyone had plates in their collection predating 1884. One such person was Jeff Francis, a former president of the Automobile License Plate Collectors Association (ALPCA), whose collection is estimated to number approximately one million plates and is considered to be one of the most comprehensive in the world. According to Francis, he replied with a photo of an 1879 New Orleans carriage licence plate from his collection, and recalled seeing an even older plate, possibly from 1870, at some point in

★ Shahin Mohajer of Muscat, Oman, with his record for the world's largest collection of licence plates.

At the time this record was awarded in 2010, Mohajer had approximately 551 licence plates in his collection. Yes, 551, and another example of Guinness World Records failing to confirm the veracity of a licence plate record claim. Mohajer's record was eclipsed in 2011 by a couple of Hungarian brothers with 11,345 licence plates in their collection. SHAHIN MOHAJER

✱ Made of brass, this plate was obtained directly from a dealer in St. Petersburg, Russia, and is thought to be one of the oldest known "licence plates" in existence.

On the bottom left-hand side of the plate is the city seal, while the Cyrillic letter for G is stamped into the bottom right-hand side of the plate.

DICK PARKER

his travels. Another collector, Dick Parker, pointed out that ALPCA's online archives contained an image of an 1860 St. Petersburg (Russia) carriage plate from his collection. Members of the association can freely access the archives, which are generally the first port of call for any collector undertaking serious research.

The records submitted in support of the claim also came under closer scrutiny, including the newspaper records purported to confirm the use of porcelain on the city's licence plates in the 1880s. Oddly, these newspaper references did not extend beyond 1901, and in one instance even appeared to cast doubt on the claim. Under the title of "New Badges," the *Victoria Daily Colonist* reported on October 12, 1886, "the cabmen, draymen and expressmen received their new badges from the city clerk's office yesterday. The badges are 2 x 3 inches, all numbered, and are made of *tin*" [emphasis added].[11]

Guinness World Records had required that the application for the world's oldest licence plate be accompanied by a letter of support from an organization knowledgeable in the field. The obvious candidate would have been the ALPCA, as the pre-eminent licence plate organization in North America and the group to which most knowledgeable BC collectors belong. Oddly, however, this support instead came from the UK-based European Registration Plate Association (Europlate), an organization more familiar with "registration plates" of, quite naturally, Europe. When confronted with opposing information from BC collectors, Europlate conceded that it had accepted the information about the No. 6 licence plate at face value and did not have the "competence to choose between the two." The revelation of the older carriage plates from St. Petersburg and New Orleans also factored into Europlate's decision to withdraw its support for the "world record" on December 20, 2010.[12] One month later, Guinness World Records announced that it was formally retiring the oldest licence plate record category and that "there is at present no current record holder."[13] The former record holder would, however, be able to keep his certificate.

Vintage Car Collectors

For "vintage" car owners, a licence plate can be an important facet of their vehicle and is a significant component in its formal presentation at car shows and parades. In 1990, Victoria-area resident Jim Sloan purchased a 1960 Chevrolet Corvette and subsequently met its original owner, Dr. Ardeth Hasel-Gren, who had purchased it for $5,541. Hasel-Gren "had wanted a small car to do various errands in . . . [and] when she and her husband (who weighed about 300 pounds) had gone over to Vancouver to look at the car, he tried to squeeze into the driver's seat and actually got stuck behind the steering wheel right inside the Dueck showroom. They had to have a mechanic come in and remove the steering wheel in order for him to get out. She knew she had the right car!" Sloan recalled that Victoria was generally issued with low-numbered licence plates in this era and proceeded to track a five-digit plate (No. 34-091), which he now displays on the front of the car (next to the current set of Collector plates).

For Lorne Findlay, preserving the 1933 licence plates that came with his 1926 Auburn sedan has been more important than finding a Year of Manufacture plate (or YOM plates, as they are known to collectors). In 1960, Findlay was told of an old car being stored in Vancouver's Shaughnessy Heights neighbourhood. When he inquired about the car, he discovered the Auburn, which had last been used in 1934 and still sported its 1933 licence plates as well as a round temporary decal issued by the MVB to encourage motorists to keep their vehicles on the road during the Depression (by gifting them two months of free registration).

The owner, by then in his 90s, had purchased the vehicle when times were good. However, after the stock market crash of 1929, things turned sour, and he eventually lost his job to a relative of one of the company's owners. By 1934, he could no longer afford to use the car and put it away, always hoping to use it again.

When Findlay inspected the vehicle, the registration paper, which was still in the glovebox, showed that the Auburn had first been licensed in December of 1926—the same month that Findlay was born. After some negotiations he successfully acquired the car and proceeded to make it roadworthy once again.

Fifty-two years later, Findlay still has the Auburn, along with several other vintage and antique cars, while the 1933 plates hang on a wall as part of a complete collection of BC licence plates. The plates still get used on occasion, such as when a live theatre group used a 1932 REO car in a production and required 1933 plates.

★ Ken Findlay (Lorne's son) poses in front of the 1926 Auburn. **LORNE FINDLAY**

★ Jim Sloan poses with his 1960 Chevrolet Corvette. **JIM SLOAN**

As trifling as the "bun-fight" over the origins of the City of Victoria porcelain licence plates may appear, I hope that it, along with the stories in the preceding chapters, have highlighted the quirky way in which these rectangular pieces of metal tell a tale that encompasses a century of British Columbia history. As much as I enjoy collecting BC licence plates, it is the stories behind them that make them so fascinating. After all, is a licence plate with all the white paint on the numbers and letters washed off really that interesting? Not until one discovers that the reason for the missing paint likely involved hijinks by prisoners working at the Oakalla Plate Shop in 1947—which makes my 1948 BC licence plate one of my favourites (the 1952 Thunderbird and its reflection of contemporary attempts to culturally distinguish British Columbia as a tourist destination is a close second). Hopefully you, the reader, now share my enthusiasm and will look at licence plates differently. And remember, if you ever come across any old plates hanging in the garage, concealed within the wall of a house or even buried in your garden, please—for the love of plates!—think twice before discarding them. They probably have their own story to tell.

Beautiful British Columbia — THE END

BEAUTIFUL **GLOSSARY** BRITISH COLUMBIA

What to Know When Speaking about Licence Plates

BASE PLATE A licence plate which is intended to be used over multiple years and is renewed through the use of decals or tabs. For example, the flag base has been in continual use in BC since 1985 and is renewed through the use of registration decals. The 1952 (or Thunderbird) base was used for three years, with metal tabs used to renew the plates in 1953 and 1954.

DIES The design of the characters used to stamp the letters and numbers into a licence plate, used interchangeably with the word "font." Where variations occur on the same base plate, reference is made to the Die Type in order to make distinctions.

EMBOSSED The process of stamping a plate, which results in the characters being raised.

FIRST ISSUE The first year that a particular type of licence plate was issued by a jurisdiction. For example, the first issue for passenger plates in British Columbia was 1913; however, first issue Commercial Truck plates did not appear until 1936.

FLAT A licence plate that has been manufactured using computer technology that does not require embossing (or debossing) of the plates. As a result, the plates are flat.

GRAPHIC The background artwork found on a licence plate. The term is usually used to refer to a picture, logo or other design feature found on a plate.

PASSENGER A licence plate that was issued specifically for use on a private car. These are usually preferred by collectors doing a province, state or birth year run.

PRE-PROVINCIAL (PRE-STATE) The period when the Province required that motorists provide their own licence plates. In British Columbia, this was between February 29, 1904, and February 28, 1913.

PROTOTYPE Usually a plate manufactured as an example, for testing and possible regular use in the future.

RUN A collection of licence plates that covers a specific period of time or a theme. For example, a "BC run" usually refers to a collection comprising one passenger plate from each year (i.e., 1913 through to 2012 for a total of 100 plates). A "birth year run" is a licence plate from each province and state for one particular year, such as 1974.

SAMPLE Licence plates made for informational, law enforcement or hobby use. These are usually identifiable by the use of all zeros or the word SAMPLE.

SERIAL FORMAT The placement of the letters and/or numbers on a licence plate (i.e., AAA-000). Also commonly used in shorthand as either "serial" or "format."

The inspiration for this list came from Drew Steitz's website, p18s.com.

ENDNOTES

Chapter 1 THE ABC-123 OF LICENCE PLATES

1 Tim Stentiford and Christopher Garrish, "Update on World's Oldest License Plate," *Plates Magazine* 57, no. 1 (February 2011): 6.

2 Ruby Speechley, "Private Plates and Number Plates History," http://www.numberplates.com/number-plate-history.asp (June 6, 2011).

3 Luxembourg soon followed in 1895, then the German state of Baden in 1896, the Netherlands in 1898 (this was possibly the first nationally issued licence plate) and Kristiana (now Oslo) in Norway in 1899, which assigned the number A-1 to a brewery truck (Stentiford and Garrish, "Update," 8.)

4 In 1900, there were estimated to be only 700 automobiles in North America versus 10,000 in Europe. Canada, Dominion Bureau of Statistics, *Canada Yearbook, 1921* (Ottawa: F.A. Acland, King's Printer, 1922), 547.

5 The original term used by the British Columbia legislature when it passed the first act to regulate the speed and operation of vehicles in 1904 was "permit" number, but this was changed to "number plate" in 1913, when the Province assumed responsibility for issuing all licence plates. Unsure of how to refer to these new plates, the Provincial Police initially referred to them as "automobile markers" in 1913, but this never caught on and, 100 years later, "number plate" remains the proper legal definition if not the commonly recognized term. In British Columbia, drivers were not required to obtain a licence until 1925.

6 Steve Raiche, "New York," http://www.leatherlicenseplates.com/New_York.html (April 25, 2012).

7 It remains a mystery whether Prince Edward Island was issuing standardized plates at this time; Newfoundland did not start issuing them until 1920 (but would not become a Canadian province until 1949).

8 According to the lieutenant-governor's chauffeur, John Major, the first plate issued to the LG was the first in the series, and these had to be returned to the Motor Vehicle Branch when a new series was issued, such as in 1979 and 1985. Herb LeRoy, personal correspondence, July 10, 2006; see also Royal BC Museum, BC Archives, Motor Vehicle Branch Records, GR-0665, Volume 97, "General Order No. 46, November 2, 1926, Motor Vehicle Act, Paragraph 6"; and George Molecey, "Your License Plate British Columbia," *Vancouver Sun*, 1938, 5 (Magazine Section).

9 State of Delaware, "History of the License Plate," http://deldot.gov/information/media_gallery/2008/centennial_plates/license_plate_history.shtml (April 25, 2012).

10 "Cops Drive against Red-Blue Vehicle Number Plates," *Times of India*, January 13, 2012, http://articles.timesofindia.indiatimes.com/2012-01-13/ranchi/30623563_1_number-plates-fancy-number-traffic-police; see also Abhishek Chaliha, "High Security Registration Plates: All you need to know," zigwheels.com, May 4, 2012, http://www.zigwheels.com/news-features/news/high-security-registration-plates-all-you-need-to-know/12705/1.

11 Jennifer Ginn, "The Bold and the Beautiful: License Plates Do More Than Tag Cars; They Can Say a Lot about a State," *Capitol Ideas*, March/April 2012, http://www.csg.org/pubs/capitolideas/Mar_Apr_2012/statelicenseplates.aspx (March 8, 2012).

12 South Dakota, Division of Motor Vehicles, *"85 Years of History": A History of Motor Vehicle Registration and Licensing Activities in the State of South Dakota from 1905 until 1990*, July 1990, 4.

13 Ginn, "The Bold and the Beautiful."

14 AP News Archive, "Florida to Sell License Plates in Memory of Shuttle Challenger," December 30, 1986, http://www.apnewsarchive.com/1986/Florida-To-Sell-License-Plates-In-Memory-of-Shuttle-Challenger/id-439db9a8fc64198027d07bc858792bc7.

15 State of Texas, Texas Department of Transportation, *The History of Texas License Plates—80th Anniversary Edition* (Austin: Texas Department of Transportation, 1999), 81.

16 The number of plates issued by any state is difficult to determine as new designs are always being approved, while some states will annually cull poor-performing specialty plates.

17 For an excellent review of the impact that new licence plates and designs can have on the sale of existing specialty plates, see Chris O'Malley, "The Lord Taketh Away: God, Colts License Plates Slice into Sales of Charity Tags," *Indianapolis Business Review*, April 5, 2008, www.ibj.com. Other states, such as North Carolina, have recently moved to rein in the "variety of multicolor designs" used on specialty plates. Bruce Siceloff, "Road Warrior: Plate Redesign Could Be Harbinger," *News & Observer*, February 21, 2012, http://www.newsobserver.com/2012/02/21/1871628/plate-redesign-could-be-harbinger.html.

18 Loren Bloom, "Flagship Niagara License Plate," http://www.battleoflakeerieart.com/plate.php (April 25, 2012).

19 "License Plate Art a Genial Nuisance," *Eugene Register-Guardian*, February 23, 1997, 5A.

20 George Power, personal communication, October 17, 2011.

Chapter 2 PRESSING PROBLEMS

1 The gasoline used to fuel Hart's car came from a barge maintained by the Hudson's Bay Company in the harbour (they couldn't keep it in warehouses). Hart bought the company's entire 90-gallon supply, but soon regretted this as all the plumbers in town were constantly after him to sell them some for use in their blowtorches. Royal BC Museum (RBCM), BC Archives, T4289:0001 (AAAB7025), Motor vehicle licensing in British Columbia: Cecil

Clark Interview, March 4, 1987. See also Geoffrey Taylor, *The Automobile Saga of British Columbia, 1864–1914* (Victoria: Morriss Publishing, 1984), 13–14.

2   Roger Roots, "The Orphaned Right: The Right to Travel by Automobile, 1890–1950," *Oklahoma City University Law Review* 30 (July 2005): 256.

3   British Columbia, Section 7 (Rate of speed), An Act to Regulate the Speed and Operation of Motor Vehicles on Highways, February 10, 1904, Chapter 41 (Victoria: King's Printer): 236.

4   Royal BC Museum, BC Archives, Cecil Clark Interview, 1987.

5   Quoted in Margaret Ormsby, *British Columbia: A History* (Toronto: Macmillan Company of Canada Limited, 1958), 342.

6   Tony Cashman, *A History of Motoring in Alberta* (Edmonton: Spartan Press, 1976), 8.

7   RBCM, BC Archives, Cecil Clark Interview, 1987.

8   Ibid.

9   RBCM, BC Archives, Motor Vehicle Branch Records, GR-0665, Volume 85, Correspondence, Superintendent Colin Campbell to the Thomas Smith (Chief Constable, Vancouver), January 9, 1913.

10 Ibid., Superintendent Colin Campbell to William Parkinson (Chief Constable, Edmonds), February 8, 1913.

11 The full correspondence can be found at RBCM, BC Archives, Motor Vehicle Branch Records, GR-0665, Volume 85, Correspondence, Superintendent Colin Campbell to Secretary of State (Oregon), June 18, 1913; and to Secretary of State (Washington), June 18, 1913; to Harry Woods (Secretary of State, Illinois), July 5, 1913; to the Deputy Provincial Secretary (Alberta), July 25, 1914; and to the McClary Manufacturing Company, July 28, 1913.

12 RBCM, BC Archives, Motor Vehicle Branch Records, GR-0665, Volume 86, Correspondence, Colin Campbell, Superintendent of Provincial Police, to George Scott, MacDonald Manufacturing Company Limited, August 24, 1914; and to George Scott, MacDonald Manufacturing Company Limited, September 5, 1914.

13 RBCM, BC Archives, Cecil Clark interview, 1987.

14 "Tacey & Sons Plan New Sheet Metal Factory," *British Columbia Record*, July 26, 1920, 2.

15 "Tories Opposed to Prison Auto Plates," *Vancouver Province*, January 11, 1930, 1.

16 See "Auto Plates to Be Made at Oakalla," *Vancouver Sun*, January 10, 1930, 1, 20; "Tories Opposed to Prison Auto Plates," *Vancouver Province*, January 11, 1930, 1; "Defends Giving Work to Oakalla," *Vancouver Province*, January 12, 1930, 2; "Unions Deny Jail Labor Approval," *Vancouver Sun*, January 13, 1930, 14; "To Wind Up Department of Industries," *Victoria Daily Colonist*, February 12, 1930, 11.

17 "No Award for Worker Injured," *Vancouver Sun*, February 11, 1930, 3, 11.

18 Ron Marston, personal communication, October 25, 2011; Keith Jackman, personal correspondence, October 31, 2011.

19 Yukon Government, Yukon Archives, GOV2654, File Nos. 1 & 2, Records Office Files, Correspondence, J.D. Gibbs (Business Manager, Oakalla), to H.J. Taylor (Territorial Secretary, Yukon), September 27, 1965.

20 See "Fore-and-Aft Licences Return to B.C. Monday," *Victoria Daily Colonist*, January 28, 1948, 1; "Gremlin Enters Licence Plate Paint," *Vancouver Province*, February 12, 1948, 2; "Sabotage of 'Plates' Suggested," *Vancouver Province*, February 25, 1948, 1; "100,000 New Car Plates Needed to Replace Duds," *Vancouver News Herald*, February 27, 1948, 3; and "200 'Peeled' Plates Traded Every Day," *Vancouver Province*, April 1, 1948, 31.

21 See "Mystery of the Peeling Numbers," *Vancouver Province*, February 8, 1949, 4; "Sabotage of 'Plates' Suggested," *Vancouver Province*, February 25, 1948, 1; "100,000 New Car Plates Needed to Replace Duds," *Vancouver News Herald*, February 27, 1948, 3; and "B.C. Not Only Victim of Licence Plate Rash," *Victoria Daily Colonist*, March 31, 1948, 19.

22 See "1949 Car Plates 'Won't Peel,' Hood," *Vancouver Sun*, November 29, 1948, 3; "No Peeling Problem for 1949 Auto License Plates: Official," *Vancouver Sun*, January 31, 1949, 6.

23 "B.C. Not Only Victim of Licence Plate Rash," *Victoria Daily Colonist*, March 31, 1948, 19.

24 Kayce White, "Lost Keys and Returned Vets," *BC Motorist*, March–April, 1966, 26–7.

25 Joe Sallman, "War Veterans Key Chain Tags," http://www.canplates.com/keychain.html (November 2, 2011).

26 Ron Marston, personal communication, July 14, 2009.

27 Dave Barrett and William Miller, *Barrett: A Passionate Political Life* (Vancouver: Douglas & McIntyre, 1995), 16, 25–26.

28 Jim Hutson, "Three of a Kind," *Vehicle* 18, no. 10 (July 1996): 3.

29 Keith Jackman, personal communication, June 5, 2008; Ron Marston, personal communication, July 14–15, 2009.

30 Keith Jackman, personal communication, November 4, 2011.

31 The Restraint program represented an attempt by the Bennett administration to reduce the size and scope of the provincial government through significant budgetary cuts and program elimination.

32 Keith Jackman, personal communication, October 16, November 4, 2011; George Piva, personal communication, October 18, 2011. With a "close registered graphic," the colours come close but don't touch.

33 George Piva, personal communication, October 18, 2011.

34 Information on the Rangers is based on the work of Whitney Lackenbauer, "Guerrillas in Our Midst: The Pacific Coast Militia Rangers, 1942–45," *BC Studies*, no. 155 (Autumn, 2005): 31–67.

35 See "'Bugs' Hold Up Delivery of New Plates," *Victoria Times Colonist*, January 25, 1985, A1; "New Licence Plates Ready but Withheld for Another 10 Days," *Victoria Times Colonist*, February 27, 1985, C9; and "B.C. Stacks New Licence Plates," *Victoria Times Colonist*, May 2, 1985, B9. Also, Keith Jackman, personal communication, October 16, 2011; George Piva, personal communication, October 18, 2011.

36 George Piva, personal communication, October 18, 2011. According to Piva, Astrographic has been able to make the same profitability in graphics volumes on an order worth $600,000 as it would have made on a licence plate contract with the Province valued at $2 million.

37 "Sask. Licence Plates to Be Made in N.S.," Canadian Broadcasting Corporation, August 18, 2010, www.cbc.ca.

38 "SGI Eyes N.S. Firm to Make Licence Plates," *Regina Leader-Post*, August 19, 2010, www.canada.com.

Chapter 3   "JUMBLED FREAK"

1 Office of the Prime Minister, "Notes for an Address," Stephen Harper, Prime Minister of Canada, Victoria, British Columbia, February 11, 2010, http://www.scribd.com/doc/26742680/Stephen-Harper-s-Speech-to-B-C-Legislature-Feb-10-2010.

2 Anonymous, "Change British Columbia's Slogan: The Best Place on Earth," Petition Online, http://www.petitiononline.com/bcslogan/petition.html (December 17, 2011).

3 Jonathon Leib, "Identity, Banal Nationalism, Contestation, and North American License Plates," *The Geographical Review* 101, no. 1 (January 2011): 39.

4 New Jersey used markers in 1908 and 1909 to validate its licence plates, but the design of these was a nondescript circle. See also Keith Sculle and John Jakle, "Signs in Motion: A Dynamic Agent in Landscape and Place," *Journal of Cultural Geography* 25, no. 1 (February 2008): 64.

5 It is rumoured that the registrar was fired before the cod was able to appear on regular passenger plates. Chris Woodcock, "Chris Woodcock's Massachusetts License Plates," http://www.w-a.com/maplate.htm (November 24, 2011). See also Massachusetts Department of Transportation, "History of the Plate," http://www.mass.gov/rmv/history/ (May 24, 2012).

6 Tim Sultan, "Vintage Cars, Vintage Plates," *New York Times*, May 6, 2005, http://www.nytimes.com/2005/05/06/automobiles/06plates.html?_r=1&pagewanted=1.

7 "Licence Plates May Advertise Timber of B.C.," *Victoria Daily Colonist*, February 20, 1929, 1.

8 Dave Hollins, personal communication, June 16, 2002.

9 "Plan to Adopt B.C. Emblem May Be Revived," *Vancouver Province*, April 12, 1948, 12; "What

about Permanent Licence Plates?" *Vancouver Province*, November 26, 1948, 4; and "Where Are Those Permanent Plates?" *Vancouver Province*, April 12, 1949, 4.

10 Michael Dawson, *Selling British Columbia: Tourism and Consumer Culture, 1890–1970* (Vancouver: UBC Press, 2004), 155, 166.

11 The number of passenger vehicles registered in 1945 was approximately 99,421. By 1950, the figure had increased to 198,397. Report of the Superintendent of Motor-Vehicles, 1950, MM7.

12 See "Permanent License Plates for B.C. Cars Subject of Survey," *Victoria Times*, September 27, 1949, 15; "Five-Year License Plates, Drivers' Licenses for B.C.," *Vancouver Sun*, March 18, 1950, 1; "Five-Year Licences Scheduled for 1951," *Victoria Daily Colonist*, March 18, 1950, 1; "Motorists Won't Get New Plates," *Vancouver Province*, March 29, 1950, 1; "B.C. Considers Five-Year Licence Plates," *Vancouver Province*, March 31, 1950, 3; "Same Licenses, New Tabs on Cars in 1951," *Victoria Times*, July 14, 1950, 1; "Put Our Totem Poles to Work," *Vancouver Province*, July 11, 1950, 4; "Group Wants Totem on B.C. Car Plates," *Vancouver Province*, July 29, 1950, 17; "Thunderbird on New B.C. License Plate," *Vancouver Sun*, August 14, 1950, 1; "Totem Figures to Be Printed On Car Plates," *Victoria Daily Colonist*, August 15, 1950, 14; "For a Licence Plate Program," *Vancouver News Herald*, August 15, 1951, 4; "What Does a Thunderbird Mean?" *Victoria Daily Colonist*, September 8, 1951, 4; and "Totem License Jumbled Freak," *Vancouver Sun*, February 23, 1953, 4.

13 "Making a Mess of B.C. License Plates," *Vancouver News Herald*, September 6, 1951, 4.

14 See "What Does a Thunderbird Mean," *Daily Colonist*, September 8, 1951, 4; "Putting Our Totem on the Road," *Vancouver Province*, September 14, 1951, 4; "Totem License Jumbled Freak," *Vancouver Sun*, February 23, 1953, 4; "Study Launched Of License Tabs," *Daily Colonist*, March 21, 1953, 5; "B.C. Abandons Car License Tab System," *Victoria Times*, August 6, 1953, 1; "Car License Aluminum Up for Sale," *Victoria Times*, August 8, 1953, 5; and "'Totemland' Legend Pushed For B.C. Car Licenses," *Victoria Times*, February 10, 1954, 26.

15 "New Licence Plate Color 'Horrible,'" *Vancouver Province*, January 20, 1955, 10.

16 "'Horrible' Plates Fail to Upset Drivers," *Vancouver Province*, January 22, 1955, 9.

17 See "Licence Plate Snafu Can't Be Corrected," *Victoria Times*, February 7, 1957, 2; and "Licence Plates May Not Mix," *Victoria Daily Colonist*, February 8, 1957, 15.

18 "Indistinct Licence Plates," *Victoria Daily Colonist*, January 11, 1958, 4; see also "New Licence Plates Too Hard to See," *Victoria Daily Colonist*, January 9, 1958, 19.

19 "Green and Gold—And Weak Pea Soup," *Vancouver Province*, March 5, 1958, 4.

20 "Licence Plates in '58 to Be Green on Gold," *Victoria Daily Colonist*, October 6, 1956, 26; see also British Columbia Centennial Committee, *The Report of the British Columbia Centennial Committee* (Vancouver: Mitchell Press), 1959, 14.

21 Joseph P. Sallmen, *Ontario License Plates: A Century of History* (Self-Published, 2004), 13.

22 "Licence Plates' Blush Dreamed Up 'Back East,'" *Victoria Daily Colonist*, January 6, 1961,

13; "You'll Get Used to Them—Time Heals Everything!" *Victoria Times*, January 6, 1961, 13; "Exciting, Exotic Exults AAA," *Victoria Times*, January 10, 1961, 11; "B.C. Puts Beauty, Color on New Licence Plates," *Victoria Daily Colonist*, August 30, 1962, 1.

23 "Blue Plate Special for Cars Next Year," *Victoria Times*, August 30, 1962, 17; and "Blue, White, Year in, Out," *Vancouver Sun*, September 16, 1963, 2.

24 "Trade Board Objects to Slogan on Licence," *Vancouver Province*, January 3, 1958, 2; and "Long Live the License Plate," *Vancouver Province*, February 6, 1964, 4.

25 Yukon Government, Yukon Archives, GOV 2653, File Nos. 6–8, Records Office Files, Correspondence, W.A. Macdonald (Planning Branch, National Centennial Commission) to the Commissioner of the Yukon Territory, February 17, 1964.

26 "Licence Plates Get Red Look for One Year," *Vancouver Province*, November 9, 1966, 25.

27 See Leib, "Identity, Banal Nationalism," 40–41; "A Contest for Slogan on Plates," *Deseret News*, November 10, 1981, 4; and Scott Christensen and John Clark, "Utah: This Is the Plate," *Plates* 54, no. 3 (June 2008): 22–23.

28 "Letters Coming on Plates," *Victoria Daily Colonist*, November 8, 1966, 37; "Car Plates Alter," *Vancouver Sun*, November 8, 1966, 19.

29 Ron Marston, personal correspondence, August 26, 2010; October 22, 2011.

30 Donald E. Knuth, "Mathematical Vanity Plates," *The Mathematical Intelligencer* 33, no. 1 (2011): 34; Ron Marston, personal correspondence, July 1, 2009.

31 Leib, "Identity, Banal Nationalism," 38–48.

32 Bob Plecas, *Bill Bennett: A Mandarin's View* (Vancouver: Douglas & McIntyre, 2006), 183.

33 Keith Jackman, personal communication, October 16, 2011; George Piva, personal communication, October 18, 2011.

34 Leib, "Identity, Banal Nationalism," 39.

35 George Piva, personal communication, October 18, 2011.

36 "ICBC: Province running out of six-character licence plate numbers," News 1130, May 25, 2010, http://www.news1130.com/news/local/article/58963--icbc-province-running-out-of-six-character-licence-plate-numbers.

37 Pierre Delacôte, personal communication, November 2, 2010.

Chapter 4 THE ROAD TO A PERMANENT PLATE

1 "Do We Want Permanent Licence Plates?" *Vancouver Province*, January 27, 1948, 4; "We'll Remember Them Now," *Vancouver Sun*, November 17, 1969. 4.

2   "Seek Elimination of New Car Plates," *Vancouver Province*, January 19, 1942, 8.

3   British Columbia, Provincial Police, Report of the Provincial Police, 1933 (Victoria: King's Printer, 1934), 29.

4   "Do We Want Permanent Licence Plates?" *Vancouver Province*, January 27, 1948, 4. See also "Why Not Permanent Numbers for Motor Vehicles?" *Victoria Daily Colonist*, September 19, 1948, 4; and "What about Permanent Licence Plates?" *Vancouver Province*, November 26, 1948, 4; "Where Are Those Permanent Plates?" *Vancouver Province*, April 12, 1949, 4; RBCM, BC Archives, Motor Vehicle Branch Records, GR-0665, Volume 97, Motor Vehicle Circular No. 164, January 23, 1933; "Permanent License Plates for B.C. Autos under Study," *Vancouver Sun*, September 26, 1949, 1.

5   British Columbia, Motor Vehicle Branch, Annual Report of the Superintendent of Motor-Vehicles for the Year 1950 (Victoria: King's Printer, 1951), MM8.

6   "'Use Again' Plates for B.C. Autos," *Vancouver Sun*, February 18, 1950, 1.

7   Archie Steacy and Sharel Fraser, personal communication, October 18, 2011; Stephen Johansen, "Behind the Scenes: Designing the Vet Plates," *Vehicle* 26, no. 18 (November 12, 2004): 2.

8   "Accomplishing the 'Impossible,'" *Vancouver Province*, July 18, 1950, 4.

9   "Licence Tabs Have Taboo," *Vancouver Province*, February 6, 1951, 8; and "Car Strips Pose Problems for Police," *Victoria Daily Colonist*, February 22, 1951, 6.

10 "Local Man Invents Lightup Licence Plate," *Vancouver Province*, October 15, 1949, 2. See also L.J. Walshe, U.S. Patent No. 1,381,038, "License Number Plate and Tail Light," patented June 7, 1921; "BC Offered New-Type Licenses," *Vancouver News Herald*, February 3, 1950, 3.

11 "Easy-to-Remove Tabs Already Disappearing," *Vancouver Province*, March 7, 1953, 9; "Study Launched of Licence Tabs," *Victoria Daily Colonist*, March 21, 1953, 5; "License Plate Problem," *Victoria Times*, March 23, 1953, 4; "B.C. Abandons Car License Tab System," *Victoria Times*, August 6, 1953, 1; "Aluminum Licence Plate System to Be Discarded," *Vancouver Province*, August 6, 1953, 1.

12 Yukon Government, Yukon Archives, GOV 2654, File Nos. 1 & 2, Records Office Files, Correspondence, J.D. Gibbs (Business Manager, Oakalla Prison) to H.J. Taylor (Territorial Secretary), September 27, 1965; and GOV 2653, File Nos. 6–8, Correspondence, J.D. Gibbs (Business Manager, Oakalla Prison) to H.J. Taylor (Registrar of Motor Vehicles), April 29, 1964.

13 BC Stats, "British Columbia Licensed Passenger Vehicles as at December 31," February 2011, http://www.bcstats.gov.bc.ca/data/dd/handout/mvlic.pdf.

14 "We Get Letters, Maybe, on Plates," *Victoria Times*, November 8, 1966, 2.

15 "Lifetime Plates for Vintage Cars," *Victoria Daily Colonist*, February 19, 1966, 17; "Antique Plates," *Vancouver Province*, February 19, 1966, 10; "Permanent Plates for Old Cars," *Victoria Times*, February 19, 1966, 35.

16 Ron Marston, personal communication, October 22, 2011; "We Get Letters, Maybe, on Plates," *Victoria Times*, November 8, 1966, 2; "Letters, Long-Life Plates Coming for Cars in 1970," *Victoria Daily Colonist*, March 1, 1969, 1.

17 Donald E. Knuth, "Mathematical Vanity Plates," *The Mathematical Intelligencer* 33, no. 1 (2011): 34.

18 The initial block of one million plates started at AAA-001 and ran through to KKJ-999 (KKK was not issued because it was one of the letter combinations deemed inappropriate by the MVB). So, instead of progressing from AAK-999 to AAL-000, the lettering rolled over and would have started at ABA-000. To meet the anticipated demand for the remainder of the year and 1972, the MVB issued a smaller allotment of plates starting at KLL-000 and running through KXX-999. See Motor Vehicle Branch, "1970 Plate Allotment List"; "M.V.B. 1971 Allotment"; and "1972 Allotment," www.BCpl8s.ca (September 27, 2011).

19 Peter Hill, personal communication, June 25, 2011.

20 Norm Gaumont and Dave Babineau, "The Role of Automatic License Plate Recognition Technology in Policing: Results from the Lower Mainland of British Columbia," *The Police Chief* 65, no. 11 (November 2008), http://policechiefmagazine.org/magazine/index.cfm?fuseaction=display&article_id=1671&issue_id=112008. See also Irwin Cohen, Darryl Plecas and Amanda McCormick, *A Report on the Utility of the Automated Licence Plate Recognition System in British Columbia*, University College of the Fraser Valley, 2007, http://www.ufv.ca/Assets/CCJR/CCJR+Resources/CCJR+Publications/ALPR.pdf.

21 Gaumont and Babineau, "The Role of Automatic License Plate Recognition."

22 Ibid.

23 "ICBC Issues New Permits for Plates," *Victoria Times*, September 27, 1974, 19.

24 Martin Cassidy, "DMV Becomes Unglued: Registration Stickers Eliminated after 70 Years," *Stamford Advocate*, July 15, 2010, http://www.stamfordadvocate.com/local/article/DMV-becomes-unglued-Registration-stickers-579041.php.

25 Rob Termuende, personal communication, October 19, 2011.

26 George Power, personal communication, October 17, 2011.

Chapter 5 WE'RE NOT SO VAIN, ARE WE?

1 Kevin Burke, "James Michael Curley and the #5 License Plate," *Jamaica Plain Historical Society*, http://www.jphs.org/people/2005/4/14/james-michael-curley-and-the-5-license-plate.html (December 29, 2009).

2 RBCM, BC Archives, Motor Vehicle Branch Records, GR-0665, Volume 89; and "Government Has No. 1 License: First Auto Plate Reserved for Official Use This Year," *Victoria Times*,

3   "'Think of a Number' And Try and Get It," *Victoria Times*, February 24, 1940, 13.

4   RBCM, BC Archives, Motor Vehicle Branch Records, GR-0665, Volume 89, Correspondence, W.H. Malkin to Superintendent of Provincial Police, November 30, 1929; Secretary to the Minister of Finance to Superintendent of Provincial Police, December 2, 1929; D.H. Meyer to Superintendent of Provincial Police, December 26, 1929. See also "Government Has No. 1 License: First Auto Plate Reserved for Official Use This Year," *Victoria Times*, February 16, 1938, 1.

5   "Government Has No. 1 License: First Auto Plate Reserved for Official Use This Year," *Victoria Times*, February 16, 1938, 1.

6   Robin Fisher, *Duff Pattullo of British Columbia* (Toronto: University of Toronto Press, 1991), 199.

7   "Car Owners Have Two Weeks to Seek Special Licence Plates," *Victoria Daily Colonist*, January 18, 1947, 1.

8   Ian Street, "'Snob' Plates Doomed?" *Vancouver Province*, December 23, 1966, 5.

9   Donald E. Knuth, "Mathematical Vanity Plates," *The Mathematical Intelligencer* 33, no. 1 (2011): 33; Tim Stentiford, "Vanity: Born in the USA", *Plates* 54, no. 4 (August 2008): 22–23; Caroline Dipping, "Avid volunteer got state's first vanity plate in '70," *San Diego Union-Tribune*, July 8, 2011, http://www.utsandiego.com/news/2011/jul/08/avid-volunteer-got-states-first-vanity-plate-70/.

10   "MLA Wants Personalized Car Plates," *Vancouver Province*, March 6, 1959, 26; "BC to Issue 5-Year Car Plates," *Vancouver News Herald*, December 19, 1951, 1; "Totem Motif to Disappear From Licences," *Vancouver Province*, August 13, 1953, 3.

11   "We Get Letters, Maybe, on Plates," *Victoria Times*, November 8, 1966, 2; "Letters Coming on Plates," *Daily Colonist*, November 8, 1966, 37; "New Licence," *Vancouver Province*, November 8, 1966, 1; "Car Plates Alter: To Show Letters," *Vancouver Sun*, November 8, 1966, 19.

12   "Odd Requests for Special Numbers on Licence Plates Are Received," *Daily Colonist*, February 1, 1946, 13; and Ian Street, "'Snob' Plates Doomed?" *Vancouver Province*, December 23, 1966, 5.

13   "Letters, Long-Life Plates Coming for Cars in 1970," *Victoria Colonist*, March 1, 1969, 1–2.

14   Keith Jackman, personal communication, June 22, 2009.

15   "Drivers Angry about Letters on New Plates," *Victoria Daily Colonist*, January 3, 1973, 9; "Some See Stigma in Car Letters," *Victoria Times*, January 3, 1973, 19.

16   Bruce Roger, personal communication, November 29, 2009. See also "Calling 007: Find Out Who Pirated 001, 002," *Victoria Times*, January 6, 1970, 13; "Triple Zero Thickens Plates Plot," *Victoria Daily Colonist*, January 7, 1970, 17.

17 "Personalized in B.C.," *Victoria Times*, April 28, 1979, 2; "Bennett Considers Ego Plates," *Vancouver Sun*, May 16, 1978, A1.

18 "3,000 Taboos for 'Vanity' Plates," *Victoria Times*, June 27, 1979, 1, 16.

19 Keith Jackman, personal communication, March 28, 2009.

20 "Few Seek Vanities," *Victoria Times*, August 22, 1979, 7.

21 "Design Snarl Delays Plates," *Vancouver Sun*, October 11, 1979, A11.

22 Keith Jackman, personal communication, March 29, 2009; "3,000 Taboos for 'Vanity' Plates," *Victoria Times*, June 27, 1979, 1, 16.

23 "B.C. Dishes Up Ego on a Plate," *Victoria Daily Colonist*, December 6, 1979, 1.

24 Keith Jackman, personal communication, March 29, 2009.

25 Aileen Campbell, "If You Have a Taste for It Fine, but Don't Ask for Too Much on Your Plate This Year, Please," *Vancouver Province*, January 7, 1980, A4.

26 Keith Jackman, personal communication, March 29, 2009; George Power, personal communication, October 17, 2011.

27 "ICBC Chops Logger Logo," *Vancouver Province*, September 5, 1993, A5.

28 Marybeth Herald, "Licensed to Speak: The Case of Vanity Plates," *University of Colorado Law Review* 72 (2001): 595–662.

29 Frank Nuessel, "License Plate Language," *American Speech* 57, no. 4 (1982): 256–59.

30 George Power, personal communication, October 17, 2011.

31 Joe Kafka, "Bill Would Dump Vanity License Plates in S.D.," *Rapid City Journal*, January 6, 2008, http://rapidcityjournal.com.

32 Rob Teremuende, personal communication, October 21, 2011.

33 Jeff Biddle, "A Bandwagon Effect in Personalised License Plates," *Economic Enquiry* 29, no. 2 (1991): 379.

34 Mily Ramshaw and Amy Rosen, "State Official, Competing Firms Spar over Texas' Specialty License Plate Business," *Dallas Morning News*, February 10, 2008, http://www.dallasnews.com.

Chapter 6   THE COST OF PROVINCE BUILDING

1 Mel Rothenburger, *Friend o' Mine: The Story of Flyin' Phil Gaglardi* (Victoria: Orca, 1991), 110.

2 Geoffrey Taylor, *The Automobile Saga of British Columbia: 1864–1914* (Victoria: Morriss Publishing, 1984), 113–15.

3   Rothenburger, *Friend o' Mine*, 111.

4   Martin Robin, *Pillars of Profit: The Company Province 1934–1972* (Toronto: McClelland & Stewart, 1973), 192. See also Rothenburger, *Friend o' Mine*, 111.

5   W.A.C. Bennett, quoted in Robin, *Pillars of Profit*, 193–94.

6   David Mitchell, *W.A.C. Bennett and the Rise of British Columbia* (Vancouver: Douglas & McIntyre, 1983), 260. See also Rothenburger, *Friend o' Mine*, 111.

7   Mitchell, *W.A.C. Bennett*, 261.

8   H.F. Angus et al., *Report of the Commission of Inquiry into Road-User Charges* (Victoria: Queen's Printer, 1959), 11.

9   Ibid., 7.

10 Ibid., 13–56.

11 Jeanette Taylor, *River City: A History of Campbell River and the Discovery Islands* (Madeira Park, BC: Harbour, 1999), 159–60.

12 Arthur Mayse, quoted in ibid., 159–60.

13 Angus et al., *Report of the Commission*, 21; H.F. Angus et al., *Report of the 1960 (Second) Commission of Inquiry into Road-User Charges* (Victoria: Queen's Printer, November 1960), 9–21.

14 "Logging Group Asks Repeal of New B.C. Transport Act," *Vancouver Sun*, February 20, 1960, 20.

15 "Truck Taxes under Fire by Socreds," *Vancouver Sun*, February 24, 1960, 25.

16 Angus et al., *Report of the 1960 (Second) Commission*, 10.

17 Automotive Transport Association of B.C., "Reply of Automotive Transport Association of B.C.," February 8, 1960, 3–8.

18 Ibid., 3–8, 35.

19 Angus et al., *Report of the Commission*, 5–7, 46,

20 Automotive Transport Association of British Columbia, "Submission to the Royal Commission," April 27, 1960, 2–3, 21.

21 Patrick J. Foley, Special Assistant to the Secretary of State of Michigan, letter to Automotive Association of British Columbia, June 8, 1959, quoted in ibid., 13.

22 Alberta had embraced reciprocity, and by 1960 it had negotiated agreements with 29 states. Noted in Automotive Association of British Columbia, "Brief on Reciprocity and Pro-Rationing," submitted to the Minister of Commercial Transport, the Honourable Lyle Wicks, April 27, 1960, 20.

23 Angus et al. *Report of the Commission*, 47; Angus et al., *Report of the 1960 (Second) Commission*, 20.

24 Angus et al., *Report of the 1960 (Second) Commission*, 24.

25 British Columbia made the agreement by order-in-council 2465, approved September 26, 1961, and published in the Gazette as B.C. Reg 151/61. Luigi Di Marzo, "Legal Status of Agreement Concluded by Component Units of Federal States with Foreign Entities," *Canadian Yearbook of International Law 1978*, Volume 16 (1978): 216n60.

26 Anonymous, "The International Registration Plan," *The Common Interest*, thecommoninterest.org/docs/Trans/ITA%20Introduction%20to%20IRP.doc (August 25, 2011).

27 Ibid.

28 Of equal significance, the US Congress had mandated that all states join the plan by September 30, 1996, or lose the ability to regulate commercial vehicles and the fees that went along with that. Anonymous, The International Registration Plan. See also Paul Teske et al., *Deregulating Freight Transportation: Delivering the Goods* (Lanham, MD: American Enterprise Institute Press, 1995), 169.

29 Ibid.

30 Article VI (Credentials) of the Plan specifically states that "upon the registration of an Apportionable Vehicle under the Plan, the Base Jurisdiction shall issue a Cab Card and a Plate for the Vehicle, and these shall be the sole registration Credentials issued for the Vehicle. The Plate shall be identified by having the word 'apportioned,' 'APP,' or 'PRP' and the name of the Base Jurisdiction. The numbering system and color of the Plate shall be determined by the Base Jurisdiction."

31 "Should Road Users Pay More?" *Financial Post*, March 25, 1961, 69.

32 Union of British Columbia Municipalities (UBCM), "A Brief of the Remarks of Counsel for the Union of British Columbia Municipalities Made to the Standing Committee of the Legislature of British Columbia on Municipal Matters on Friday, March 2nd, 1962, with Regard to the Licensing of Commercial Motor Vehicles by Municipal Governments," 5.
See also Angus at al., *Report of the 1960 (Second) Commission*, 25.

33 Construction Equipment Owners Association of B.C., "Submission to Standing Legislative Committee on Municipal Matters," March 2, 1962, 4.

34 Ibid., 25.

35 Ibid., 12.

36 Automotive Transport Association of BC, Submission to the Royal Commission, August 1960, 13.

37 Construction Equipment Owners Association of B.C., "Submission to Standing Legislative Committee on Municipal Matters," March 2, 1962, 12.

38 RBCM, BC Archives, Motor Vehicle Branch Records, GR-0665, Volume 97, J.H. McMullen, MVB Circular No. 90, March 21, 1930; "New Letters on Car Plates," *Victoria Times*, February 8, 1938, 1; "Dope Precaution", *Vancouver Province*, April 28, 1944, 19.

39 Automotive Transport Association of BC, Submission to the Royal Commission, August 1960, 13–19.

40 Angus et al. *Report of the 1960 (Second) Commission*, 27.

41 UBCM, "A Brief of the Remarks of Counsel" 6–18.

42 "Should Road Users Pay More?" *Financial Post*, March 25, 1961, 70.

43 Report of the Department of Municipal Affairs, 1962, X11; Report No. 1, Legislative Committee Room, March 23, 1962, Select Standing Committee on Municipal Matters, 150–51.

44 It is estimated that approximately 24 percent of the revenue generated by the program is required to cover the administrative costs incurred by the UBCM in administering the program. In 2008, this left slightly more than $800,000 to be disbursed amongst the 102 participating municipalities. BC Trucking Association, Briefing Note, "UBCM CVL Program Submission," March 23, 2008; "Fines on the Rise in BC for Failure to Display Municipal Decals," *Today's Trucking*, November 12, 2007, http://www.todaystrucking.com/printarticle.cfm?intDocID=18824.

Chapter 7 IN THE INTERESTS OF THE TRAVELLING PUBLIC

1 Kenneth Button and Garland Chow, "Road Haulage Regulation: A Comparison of the Canadian, British and American Approaches," *Transport Reviews* 3, no. 3 (1983): 239.

2 "Drayage" refers to the transportation of goods over a short distance by truck, usually from a railway yard or shipping wharf to a warehouse. William Thomas, "Rollin' on . . . to a Free Market—Motor Carrier Regulation 1935–1980," *Transportation Law Journal* 13 (1984), 44–45.

3 Canada, Dominion Bureau of Statistics, *The Canada Year Book, 1922–23: Official Statistical Annual of the Resources, History, Institutions and Social and Economic Conditions of the Dominion* (Ottawa: F.A. Acland, King's Printer, 1924), 649.

4 Timothy Brady, *A History of Trucking Regulation 1880–1949*, http://www.getloaded.com/content/history-trucking-regulation-1880-1949-part-1 (August 17, 2010).

5 Canada, Dominion Bureau of Statistics, *The Canada Year Book, 1921* (Ottawa: F.A. Acland, King's Printer, 1922), 547–48; *The Canada Year Book, 1922–23*, 671. See also Thomas, "Rollin' on," 46.

6 Dorothy Robyn, *Braking the Special Interests: Trucking Deregulation and the Politics of Policy Reform* (Chicago: University of Chicago Press, 1987), 13; Thomas, 49; Kenneth Button and Garland Chow, "Road Haulage Regulation," 239.

7 "Four Killed in Viaduct Plunge," *Vancouver Sun*, March 16, 1931, 1.

8 Thomas, "Rollin' on," 48.

9 BC Legislative Assembly, Report of the Public Utilities Commission, 1951/52, Motor Carrier Act, J14-15.

10 Michael Trebilcock et al., *Federalism and the Canadian Economic Union* (Toronto: University of Toronto Press, 1984), 247. See also Colin Hanson, Select Standing Committee on Public Accounts, February 25, 1997, http://www.leg.bc.ca/cmt/36thParl/cmt12/hansard/t12_0225.htm

11 British Columbia, Public Utilities Commission, *Annual Report of the Public Utilities Commission, Pursuant to Section 36 of the "Motor Carrier Act," for the Licence-year Ended February 28th, 1959*, Nineteenth Annual Report (Victoria: Queen's Printer, 1958/59), 3.

12 British Columbia, *Report of the Motor Carrier Commission*, 1987/88, 1.

13 "Bonner Promises Another Look on 'Ham' Plates," *Victoria Times*, March 1, 1962, 15; Dave Marshall, personal communication, September 9, 2011.

14 Hanson, Select Standing Committee on Public Accounts (see note 10 above).

15 Economic deregulation of intra-provincial raw log and gravel haulers in 2000 marked the final stage of the provincial response to federal deregulation of the freight industry. Motor Carrier Commission, *Annual Report of the Motor Carrier Commission*, February 29, 2000, 2. See also Hanson, Select Standing Committee on Public Accounts (see note 10 above).

16 British Columbia, *Report of the Motor Carrier Commission*, 1990/91, 1.

17 Ibid., 1–18.

18 Stan Lanyon et al., *A Study of the Taxi Industry in British Columbia*, Report to the Honourable Harry Lali, Minister of Transportation and Highways, June 15, 1999, 24–30.

19 Rob Nijjar, Hansard, April 22, 2004, 10385, http://www.leg.bc.ca/hansard/37th5th/h40422p.htm.

20 Passenger Transportation Board, Annual Report 2010/11, 11, http://www.th.gov.bc.ca/ptb/documents/Annual_Reports/2010_11_annual_report.pdf.

21 "Taxi Licences Deliberately Kept Low," CTV.ca, February 19, 2008, http://www.ctvbc.ctv.ca/servlet/an/plocal/CTVNews/20080219/BC_taxi_tuesday_080219/20080220/?hub=British ColumbiaHome.

Chapter 8 THE WORLD'S OLDEST LICENCE PLATE?

1 Bill Cleverley, "World's First Licence Plate Issued in Victoria in 1884," *Victoria Times Colonist*, October 19, 2010, www.timescolonist.com; Bill Cleverley, "Victoria Is the Birthplace of the Licence Plate," *Victoria Times Colonist*, October 19, 2010, www.timescolonist.com.

2 Dan Christian, personal communication, May 26, 2011.

3 "Second Plate Found," *Victoria Daily Colonist*, August 2, 1964, 16.

4 Eric Taylor, personal communication, December 10, 2010.

5   Norman Archer, "World's Oldest Licence Plates," *Senior Living Magazine*, March 1, 2010, http://www.seniorlivingmag.com/articles/worlds-oldest-licence-plates.

6   Pierre Delacôte, personal communication, October 24, 2010.

7   See City of Victoria, Bylaw No. 362 ("A By-Law Regulating Hired and Other Vehicles – Regulation of Vehicles for Hire"), adopted March 8, 1901, 259; City of Victoria, Bylaw No. 1313 ("A By-Law Regulating Hired and Other Vehicles"), adopted July 22, 1912, 1.

8   RBCM, BC Archives, GR-0665, Volume 97, Correspondence, Colin Campbell to the Secretary of State. Sacramento, California, June 18, 1913.

9   Eric Taylor, personal communication, December 10, 2010.

10 Leonora LaPeter Anton, "History on His Plate(s)," *Tampa Bay Times*, http://www.tampabay.com/features/humaninterest/article818455.ece (September 20, 2008).

11 "New Badges," *Daily Colonist*, October 12, 1886, 3.

12 Neil Park (Europlate Secretary) personal communication with Mariamarta Ruano-Graham (Guinness World Records), December 20, 2010.

13 Carim Valerio (Guinness World Records) personal communication, January 24, 2011.

LICENCE PLATE CREDITS

Unless otherwise indicated, all licence plates were photographed by Bruce Law.

Astrographic Industries Limited BC samples (p. 54), BC prototypes (p. 55), 2005 BC (p. 123).

Automobile License Plate Collectors Association 1913 Alberta (p. 40).

Graham Casey 1961 BC (p. 100).

Pierre Delacôte 1910 BC (p. 22), 1951 Royal (p. 56), 1973 BC (p. 69), 1989 BC (p. 90), 1985 BC (p. 134).

Ron Garay 1941 Georgia (p. 15), 1911 Manitoba (p. 23), 1912 Saskatchewan (p. 23), 1914 Alberta (p. 26), 1918 BC (p. 26), 1919 BC tab (p. 27), 1927 BC (p. 28), 1930 BC (p. 28), 1931 BC (p. 28), 1948 BC (p. 30), 1949 BC (p. 31), TB Vets Keytags (p. 32), 1923 Utah (p. 42), 1923 BC (p. 42), 1936 BC (p. 42), 1945 New Mexico (p. 43), 1952 BC (p. 45), 1958 BC (p. 48), 1964 BC (p. 51), 1951 BC (p. 63), 1952 BC (p. 64), 1953 BC (p. 64), 1954 BC (p. 64), 1965 BC's (p. 66), 1970 BC (p. 66), 1981 BC (p. 70), 1980 BC (p. 70), 1978 BC (p. 85), 1957 BC (p. 98), 1989 BC (p. 101), 1960 BC (p. 106), 1940 BC (p. 107), 1957 BC's (p. 118), 1973 BC (p. 118), 1974 BC (p. 118), 1963 BC (p. 119).

Christopher Garrish 1986 BC (p. 11), 1974 South Dakota (p. 15), 1976 South Carolina (p. 16), 1996 Pennsylvania (p. 17), 2010 BC (p. 17), 1948 BC (p. 30), 1986 BC (p. 36), 1963 Quebec (p. 51), 1987 BC (p. 53), 2000 BC (p. 67), 1970 BC (p. 68), 1969 BC (p. 69), 1996 BC (p. 72), 1978 BC (p. 85), 1982 BC (p. 86), 1999 BC (p. 120).

Neale Hankins 1960 Saanich (p. 107), 1962 Surrey (p. 109).

Bill Hobbis 1930 BC (p. 18), 1912 Alberta (p. 23), 1914 BC (p. 25), 1914 BC (p. 26), PCMR (p. 37), 1915 BC (p. 40), 1957 BC (p. 65), 1941 BC (p. 108), 1934 BC (p. 116).

Dave Hollins various BC (pp 2-3), 1928 Idaho (p. 15), 1947 Idaho (p. 15), 1948 Idaho (p. 15), 1958 Colorado (p. 15), 1976 Alaska (p. 16), 1976 Illinois (p. 16), 1976 Nebraska (p. 16),

1976 Hawaii (p. 16), 1976 Indiana (. 16), 1989 Florida (p. 16), 1911 Ontario (p. 23), 1913 BC (p 23), 1915 BC (p. 26), 1917 Washington (p. 26), 1910 Pennsylvania (p. 40), 1910 Michigan (p. 40), 1916 California (p. 40), 1912 Ontario (p. 40), 1912 Manitoba (p. 40), 1928 Massachusetts (p. 42), 1933 South Carolina (p. 42), 1924 BC (p. 42), 1940 Nebraska (p. 43), 1940 Wyoming (p. 43), 1945 Pennsylvania (p. 43), 1936 Tennessee (p. 43), 1951 Montana (p. 43), 1957 BC (p. 47), 1955 Saskatchewan (p. 48), 1938 Ontario (p. 48), 1951 Tennessee (p. 48), 1963 Illinois (p. 48), 1983 Manitoba (p. 48), 1959 BC (p. 49), 1960 BC (p. 49), 1961 BC (p. 49), 1962 BC (p. 49), 1978 Quebec (p. 51), undated BC (p. 52), 1944 Quebec (p. 59), 1944 Saskatchewan (p. 59), 1943 Illinois (p. 60), 1942 BC (p. 60), 1943 BC (p. 60), 1966 BC (p. 67), 1963 California (p. 68), 1996 BC (p. 72), 1993 BC's (p. 72), 1993 BC (p. 89), 1959 BC (p. 98), 1962 BC (p. 105), 1974 Bingo (p. 105), 1937 Surrey (p. 107), 1935 North Vancouver (p. 107), 1952 Delta (p. 107), 1945 New Westminster (p. 107), 1959 Richmond (p. 107), 1959 Prince George (p. 107), 1991 BC (p. 121).

Jon Olnytzky 1957 BC (p. 47), 1956 BC (p. 47), undated BC (p. 52), 1958 BC (p. 80), 1988 BC (p. 90), 1929 BC (p. 96), 1988 BC (p. 101).

Tom Lindner 1962 BC (p. 79), 1962 BC (p. 81).

John Roberts 1913 Victoria (p. 126).

Don Schneider 1991 BC (p. 91), 1927 BC (p. 116), 1930 BC (p. 116).

Phil O. Stein 1972 BC (p. 52), 1970 BC (p. 69), 1935 BC (p. 80), 1946 BC (p. 80), 1970 BC (p. 82), 1981 BC (p. 86).

BIBLIOGRAPHY

Archival Material

Royal BC Museum, BC Archives

★ T4289:0001 (AAAB7025), Motor Vehicle Licensing in British Columbia: Cecil Clark Interview, March 4, 1987.

★ GR-0664, Files Pertaining to the Start of the Insurance Corporation of British Columbia 1971–1975.

★ GR-0665, Motor Vehicle Branch Records:

  • Registers of Motor Vehicle Permits and Licences, Volumes 1 to 26;
  • Chauffeur's Licences, Volume 54;
  • Dealers Licences, Volumes 63 & 64;
  • Correspondence, Volumes 85 to 96; and
  • Motor Vehicle Circulars, Volumes 97 & 98.

★ GR-1299, Records Relating to the Royal Commission of Inquiry into Road-User Charges, Volumes 2 to 4.

★ GR-2958, Records Regarding Motor Vehicle Regulations 1916-1928.

★ MS-2661, Luney, Walter, 1881-1964. Victoria.

Yukon Archives

★ GOV 2654, Records Office Files, File Nos. 1 & 2.

★ GOV 2653, Records Office Files, File Nos. 6–8.

Interviews and Personal Correspondence

Dan Christian, Pierre Delacôte, Sharel Fraser, Greg Gibson, Adam Grossman, Peter Hill, Dave Hollins, Keith Jackman, Jeannie Lee, Herb LeRoy, Dave Marshall, Ron Marston, Andrew Osborne, Neil Park, George Piva, George Power, John Roberts, Bruce Roger, Archie Steacy, Tim Stentiford, Eric Taylor, Rob Termuende, Carim Valerio.

Books

Angus, H.F., et al. *Report of the Commission of Inquiry into Road-User Charges*. Victoria: Queen's Printer, 1959.

———. *Report of the 1960 (Second) Commission of Inquiry into Road-User Charges*. Victoria: Queen's Printer, November 1960.

Barrett, Dave, and William Miller. *Barrett: A Passionate Political Life*. Vancouver: Douglas & McIntyre, 1995.

British Columbia Centennial Committee. *The Report of the British Columbia Centennial Committee*. Vancouver: Mitchell Press, 1959.

Canada. Dominion Bureau of Statistics. *The Canada Year Book, 1921*. Ottawa: F.A. Acland (King's Printer), 1922.

———. *The Canada Year Book, 1922-23: Official Statistical Annual of the Resources, History, Institutions and Social and Economic Conditions of the Dominion*. Ottawa: F.A. Acland (King's Printer), 1924.

Cashman, Tony. *A History of Motoring in Alberta*. Edmonton: Spartan Press, 1976.

Dawson, Michael. *Selling British Columbia: Tourism and Consumer Culture, 1890-1970*. Vancouver: UBC Press, 2004.

Fisher, Robin. *Duff Pattullo of British Columbia*. Toronto: University of Toronto Press, 1991.

Hollins, Dave. "A History of British Columbia License Plates." Unpublished manuscript, 2002.

Mitchell, David. *W.A.C. Bennett and the Rise of British Columbia*. Vancouver: Douglas & McIntyre, 1983.

Ormsby, Margaret. *British Columbia: A History*. Toronto: Macmillan, 1958.

Plecas, Bob. *Bill Bennett: A Mandarin's View*. Vancouver: Douglas & McIntyre, 2006.

Reimer, Mia. "'BC at Its Most Sparkling, Colourful Best': Post-War Province Building through Centennial Celebrations." PhD diss., University of Victoria, December 2007.

Robin, Martin. *Pillars of Profit: The Company Province 1934-1972*. Toronto: McClelland & Stewart, 1973.

Rothenburger, Mel. *Friend o' Mine: The Story of Flyin' Phil Gaglardi*. Victoria: Orca, 1991.

Robyn, Dorothy. *Braking the Special Interests: Trucking Deregulation and the Politics of Policy Reform.* Chicago: University of Chicago Press, 1987.

Sallmen, Joseph. *Ontario License Plates: A Century of History.* Self-Published, 2004.

Taylor, Geoffrey. *The Automobile Saga of British Columbia, 1864-1914.* Victoria: Morriss Publishing, 1984.

Taylor, Jeanette. *River City: A History of Campbell River and the Discovery Islands.* Madeira Park, BC: Harbour Publishing, 1999.

Teske, Paul, et al. *Deregulating Freight Transportation: Delivering the Goods.* Lanham, MD: American Enterprise Institute Press, 1995.

Trebilcock, Michael, et al. *Federalism and the Canadian Economic Union.* Toronto: University of Toronto Press, 1984.

State of Texas. Texas Department of Transportation. *The History of Texas License Plates— 80th Anniversary Edition.* Austin: Texas Department of Transportation, 1999.

Weimar, Mark. *Identifying and Quantifying Rates of State Motor Fuel Tax Evasion,* Washington: National Cooperative Highway Research Program, Report No. 623, 2008.

Journal Articles

Al-Haboubi, M.H. "Designing a License Plate." *Applied Ergonomics* 30 (1999): 421-28.

Alper, Neil, Robert Archibald, and Eric Jensen. "At What Price Vanity?: An Econometric Model of the Demand for Personalized License Plates." *National Tax Journal* 40, no. 1 (March 1987): 103–9.

Biddle, Jeff. "A Bandwagon Effect in Personalised License Plates." *Economic Enquiry* 29, no. 2 (1991): 375–88.

Bryan, Nancy. "Road-User Charges in Canada." *Canadian Tax Papers*, no. 55 (1972).

Button, Kenneth, and Garland Chow. "Road Haulage Regulation: A Comparison of the Canadian, British and American Approaches." *Transport Reviews* 3, no. 3 (1983): 237–64.

Christensen, Scott, and John Clark. "Utah: This Is the Plate." *Plates: The Magazine of the Automobile License Plate Collectors Association* 54, no. 3 (June 2008): 22–23.

Colling, James. "General Lee Speaking: Are License Plate Designs Out of the State's Control? A Critical Analysis of the Fourth Circuit's Decision in Sons of Confederate Veterans, Inc. v. Comm'r of the Virginia Department of Motor Vehicles." *George Mason Law Review* 12, no. 2 (2003–2004): 441–79.

Corbin, Caroline. "Mixed Speech: When Speech is Both Private and Governmental." *New York University Law Review* 83, no. 3 (June 2008): 605–92.

Craft, Erik. "The Demand for Vanity (Plates): Elasticities, Net Revenue Maximization, and Deadweight Loss." *Contemporary Economic Policy* 20, no. 2 (April 2002): 133–44.

Di Marzo, Luigi. "Legal Status of Agreement Concluded by Component Units of Federal States with Foreign Entities." *Canadian Yearbook of International Law 1978* 16 (1978): 197-229.

Guggenheim, Jack, and Jed Silversmith. "Confederate License Plates at the Constitutional Crossroads: Vanity Plates, Special Registration Organization Plates, Bumper Stickers, Viewpoints, Vulgarity, and the First Amendment." *University of Miami Law Review* 54 (1999–2000): 563–85.

Harrington, David, and Kathy Krynski. "State Pricing of Vanity License Plates." *National Tax Journal* 42, no. 1 (March 1989): 95-99.

Herald, Marybeth. "Licensed to Speak: The Case of Vanity Plates." *University of Colorado Law Review* 72 (2001): 595–662.

Hutson, Jim. "Three of a Kind." *Vehicle* 18, no. 10 (July 12, 1996): 3.

Jacobs, Leslie Gielow. "Free Speech and the Limits of Legislative Discretion: The Example of Specialty License Plates." *Florida Law Review* 53, no. 3 (July 2001): 420–73.

Johansen, Stephen. "Behind the Scenes: Designing the Vet Plates." *Vehicle* 26, no. 18 (November 12, 2004): 1.

Knuth, Donald. "Mathematical Vanity Plates." *The Mathematical Intelligencer* 33, no. 1 (2011): 33–45.

Laband, David, Ram Pandit, and John Sophocleus. "Factors That Influence Sales of Wildlife-Related Specialty License Plates." *Human Dimensions of Wildlife* 14, no. 1 (2009): 61–70.

Lackenbauer, Whitney. "Guerrillas in Our Midst: The Pacific Coast Militia Rangers, 1942–45." *BC Studies*, no. 155 (Autumn, 2005): 31–67.

Leib, Jonathon. "Identity, Banal Nationalism, Contestation, and North American License Plates." *The Geographical Review* 101, no. 1 (January 2011): 37–52.

Ng, Travis, Terrence Chong, and Xin Du. "The Value of Superstitions." *Journal of Economic Psychology* 31 (2010): 293–309.

Nuessel, Frank. "License Plate Language." *American Speech* 57, no. 4 (1982): 256–59.

Reimer, Chad. "'Provincial in Name Only': The Great Birthday Debate of 1926 and the Early Years of the British Columbia Historical Association." *BC Historical News* 35 (Winter 2001/2002): 2–7.

Roots, Roger. "The Orphaned Right: The Right to Travel by Automobile, 1890–1950." *Oklahoma City University Law Review* 30 (July 2005): 245–69.

Sculle, Keith, and John Jakle. "Signs in Motion: A Dynamic Agent in Landscape and Place." *Journal of Cultural Geography* 25, no. 1 (February 2008): 57–85.

Stentiford, Tim. "Vanity: Born in the USA." *Plates: The Magazine of the Automobile License Plate Collectors Association* 54, no. 4 (August 2008): 21–29.

Stentiford, Tim, and Christopher Garrish. "Update on World's Oldest License Plate." *Plates: The Magazine of the Automobile License Plate Collectors Association* 57, no. 1 (February 2011): 6–10.

Thomas, William. "Rollin' On . . . To a Free Market—Motor Carrier Regulation 1935-1980." *Transportation Law Journal* 13 (1984): 44–85.

Government Reports and other Publications

BC Stats. "British Columbia Licensed Passenger Vehicles as at December 31." February 2011. http://www.bcstats.gov.bc.ca/data/dd/handout/mvlic.pdf.

———. Quarterly Population (1951-2012). http://www.bcstats.gov.bc.ca/Files/0dc3a42c-666c-4ad8-b713-18aea6d76fbb/BCquarterlypopulationestimates.csv (May 28, 2012).

Government of British Columbia. Legislative Assembly of British Columbia. *Hansard*.

———. Ministry of Social Development. "Description of the BC Mark" (Version: April 12, 2006). http://www.hsd.gov.bc.ca/wordmark/docs/for_use.pdf.

———. Protocol & Events Branch. "Consular Corps of British Columbia." http://www.protocol.gov.bc.ca/protocol/prgs/consular/consular.htm (March 12, 2012).

———. Select Standing Committee on Municipal Matters. Report No. 1. Legislative Committee Room, March 23, 1962.

———. Select Standing Committee on Public Accounts, February 25, 1997. http://www.leg. bc.ca/cmt/36thParl/cmt12/hansard/t12_0225.htm (September 18, 2011).

———. Straightforward BC. *Straightforward BC: Regulation, Clear and Simple*. http://www.tted. gov.bc.ca/sfbc/Documents/pdf/StraightforwardBC_Report.pdf (June 13, 2011).

———. Government of Alberta and Government of Saskatchewan. *New West Partnership Trade Agreement, 2011*. http://www.newwestpartnershiptrade.ca/pdf/NewWestPartnership-TradeAgreement.pdf.

Government of Canada. Office of the Prime Minister. "Notes for an Address," Stephen Harper, Prime Minister of Canada, in Victoria, British Columbia, February 11, 2010. http://www. scribd.com/doc/26742680/Stephen-Harper-s-Speech-to-B-C-Legislature-Feb-10-2010.

Government of Ontario. Ministry of Transportation. *Application for Veteran Plate Eligibility Certification*. http://www.mto.gov.on.ca/english/dandv/vehicle/veteran.pdf (November 3, 2011).

Insurance Corporation of British Columbia. *BC Licence Plate Identification Guide*, No. MV1675 (052011). 2011.

Lanyon, Stan, et al. *A Study of the Taxi Industry in British Columbia*. Report to the Honourable Harry Lali, Minister of Transportation and Highways, June 15, 1999. http://www.th.gov. bc.ca/Publications/reports_and_studies/taxi/taxi.pdf.

Websites

Abourezk, Kevin. "Did Humor Web Site Derail Online License Plate Survey?" *JournalStar. com*, May 19, 2009. http://journalstar.com/news/local/article_e02362d9-f6e5-5af8-a51a-d1b86757c224.html (20 May 2009).

American Association of Motor Vehicle Administrators. "AAMVA License Plate Legibility Testing Guidelines for Reflective Sheeting." http://www.aamva.org/aamva/DocumentDis-play.aspx?id={EBCE409A-3279-4207-9B65-C4E0C1B220B8} (January 2, 2012).

———. *Written Testimony of the American Association of Motor Vehicle Administrators on Safety and Imple-mentation Issues Associated with Increased Mexican Truck Traffic under the North American Free Trade Agreement Submitted to the Committee on Transportation & Infrastructure Subcommittee on Highways and Transit U.S. House of Representatives Washington, DC, July 17, 2001*. http://www.aamva.org/ aamva/DocumentDisplay.aspx?id=%7BDD97763D-8AC1-4CC7-9958-FCDF82432197%7D.

———. "AAMVA–LCNS2ROM™ Vanity License Plate Survey: U.S." 2007. http://www.aam-va.org/aamva/DocumentDisplay.aspx?id={FA33703E-1CFE-4797-A288-D02C3BC20781}.

Anonymous. "Change British Columbia's Slogan: The Best Place on Earth." *Petition Online*. http://www.petitiononline.com/bcslogan/petition.html (December 17, 2011).

Anonymous. "The International Registration Plan." *The Common Interest*. thecommoninterest.org/docs/Trans/ITA%20Introduction%20to%20IRP.doc (August 25, 2011).

Archer, Norman. "World's Oldest Licence Plates." *Senior Living Magazine*, March 1, 2010, http://www.seniorlivingmag.com/articles/worlds-oldest-licence-plates.

Bloom, Loren. "Flagship Niagara License Plate." *The Battle of Lake Erie Art*. http://www.battleofla-keerieart.com/plate.php (April 25, 2012).

Brady, Timothy. *A History of Trucking Regulation 1880-1949*. August 17, 2010. http://www.get-loaded.com/content/history-trucking-regulation-1880-1949-part-1.

Burke, Kevin. "James Michael Curley and the #5 License Plate." *Jamaica Plain Historical Society*. http://www.jphs.org/people/2005/4/14/james-michael-curley-and-the-5-license-plate.html (December 21, 2009).

Chaliha, Abhishek. "High Security Registration Plates: All You Need to Know." zigwheels.com, May 4, 2012. http://www.zigwheels.com/news-features/news/high-security-registration-plates-all-you-need-to-know/12705/1.

City of Richmond. "Questions & Answers on Commercial Vehicle Decals." http://www.rich-mond.ca/__shared/assets/Questions_and_Answers_on_Commercial_Vehicle_Decals_-_BL-B-19778.pdf (July 22, 2011).

City of Vancouver. Licence Office. Commercial Vehicle. "Who Needs a Commercial Vehicle Licence—Municipal Decal and/or a Commercial Vehicle Permit (Plate)?" http://vancou-ver.ca/commsvcs/licandinsp/licences/vehicle/index.htm (22 July 2011).

Cohen, Irwin, Darryl Plecas and Amanda McCormick. *A Report on the Utility of the Automated Licence Plate Recognition System in British Columbia*. University College of the Fraser Valley, 2007. http://www.ufv.ca/Assets/CCJR/CCJR+Resources/CCJR+Publications/ALPR.pdf.

Gaumont, Norm, and Dave Babineau. "The Role of Automatic License Plate Recognition Technology in Policing: Results from the Lower Mainland of British Columbia." *The Police Chief* 65, no. 11 (November 2008). http://policechiefmagazine.org/magazine/index.cfm?fuseaction=display&article_id=1671&issue_id=112008.

Ginn, Jennifer. "The Bold and the Beautiful: License Plates Do More Than Tag Cars; They Can Say a Lot about a State." *Capitol Ideas*, March/April 2012. http://www.csg.org/pubs/capi-tolideas/Mar_Apr_2012/statelicenseplates.aspx.

Lonce, Stefan. "WHZ SO VN? [WHO'S SO VAIN?]" *Move Magazine*, Fall 2007. http://www.aamva.org/Publications/Move/Fall2007/Fall2007Feat1.htm.

Ludkiewicz, Mike. *First Year of Issue Amateur Radio (Ham) Call Sign Auto License Plates.* http://www.pl8s.com/hams.htm (November 4, 2011).

Marsh, Katherine. "License to Shill." *Legal Affairs*, January/February 2003. http://www.legalaffairs.org/issues/January-February-2003/story_marsh_janfeb2003.msp.

Massachusetts Department of Transportation. Registry of Motor Vehicles. "History of the Plate." http://www.mass.gov/rmv/history/ (24 May 2012).

McDonald, Rob. "The Royal Tour Buick—Canada's Most Historic Automobile (IMHO)." Antique Automobile Club of America, ACCA Forums, February 12, 2011. http://forums.aaca.org/f165/royal-tour-buick-canadas-most-historic-298166.html.

Policinski, Gene. "The Hour May Be Late for the Vanity PL8." *First Amendment Centre*, January 13, 2008. http://www.firstamendmentcenter.org/car-talk-the-hour-may-be-late-for-the-vanity-pl8.

Raiche, Steve. "New York." http://www.leatherlicenseplates.com/New_York.html (April 25, 2012).

Sallman, Joe. "War Veterans Key Chain Tags." http://www.canplates.com/keychain.html (November 2, 2011).

Speechley, Ruby. "Private Plates and Number Plates History." http://www.numberplates.com/number-plate-history.asp (June 6, 2011).

State of California. California Environmental Protection Agency. Air Resources Board. "Key Events in the History of Air Quality in California." http://www.arb.ca.gov/html/brochure/history.htm (January 2, 2012).

State of Delaware. "History of the License Plate." http://deldot.gov/information/media_gallery/2008/centennial_plates/license_plate_history.shtml (April 25, 2012).

State of South Dakota. Division of Motor Vehicles. *"85 Years of History": A History of Motor Vehicle Registration and Licensing Activities in the State of South Dakota from 1905 until 1990.* July 1990. http://www.state.sd.us/drr2/motorvehicle/pressrelease/license%20plate%20history%2085%20years.pdf.

State of Washington. Department of Licensing. *License Plate History.* http://www.dol.wa.gov/vehicleregistration/HistoryofLicensePlates.pdf (November 24, 2011).

Swinton, John. "'Save the Manatee?' Price Elasticity of Florida's Manatee License Plate." Georgia College and State University. http://economics.gcsu.edu/papers/js03-03.pdf (June 4, 2012).

Two Way Direct Radio Products. "Glossary." http://www.twowaydirect.com/support/glossary (September 30, 2011).

Walshe, L.J. "License Number Plate and Tail Light." U.S. Patent No. 1,381,038. Patented June 7, 1921. Google Patents, www.google.com/patents (June 4, 2012).

Woodcock, Chris. "Chris Woodcock's Massachusetts License Plates." http://www.w-a.com/maplate.htm (November 24, 2011).

INDEX

To distract their young son on a cross-continental car trip, Christopher Garrish's parents encouraged him to illustrate all the different licence plates he saw. Thirty years on, Chris still finds himself scanning for plates and recording what he sees on his award-winning website, BCpl8s.ca. He has also published articles on British Columbia history in *BC Studies*, *British Columbia Historical News* and *Okanagan History*. Chris, his wife, Heather, and his two daughters —whose names can be spelled in both English and Licence Plate: K8 (Kate) and 3MM4 (Emma)—live in the Okanagan Valley.

✱ SCOTT CAMPBELL